THOMAS À BECKET,

A Tragedy;

AND

OTHER POEMS.

BY

G. H. HOLLISTER.

BOSTON:
PUBLISHED BY WILLIAM V. SPENCER,
134 WASHINGTON STREET.
1866.

Cambridge Press.
DAKIN AND METCALF.

CONTENTS.

POEMS.

PERSONS REPRESENTED.

HENRY II., *King of England.*

THOMAS À BECKET, *Chancellor of England, afterward Archbishop of Canterbury.*

PHILIP, *Pope's Legate.*

ROGER, *Archbishop of York.*

BISHOPS OF WINCHESTER, SALISBURY, *and* LONDON.

RANDOLPH DE GLANVIL, *Lord Justiciary of England.*

EARLS OF LEICESTER, CORNWALL, *and* CLARE.

JOHN, *Mareschal of the Exchequer.*

REGINALD FITZ URSE, WILLIAM DE TRACI, HUGH DE MOREVILLE, *and* RICHARD BRITO, *Gentlemen of the king's household, and murderers of Becket.*

GRIM, *Cross-bearer to Becket.*

ERNEST, *a page. An officer. A monk.*

ELEANOR OF AQUITAINE, *Queen of England.*

MATILDA, *mother of King Henry and Empress of Henry V. of Germany.*

ROSAMOND CLIFFORD, *mistress of King Henry.*

Lords, prelates, knights, gentlemen, and attendants.

THOMAS À BECKET.

ACT I.

SCENE I. — *A room in Westminster Palace.*

Enter GLANVIL, *Chief Justiciary of England, and* ROGER, *Archbishop of York.* TIME — *Evening.*

YORK. Welcome, de Glanvil! Is the rumor true
That Henry's low-born Saxon chancellor,
Archdeacon Becket, shall be England's primate,
And I shall kneel to him?

GLAN. Becket, my Lord?

YORK. Ay, 'tis so whispered. Is it news to thee?

GLAN. It cannot be that Henry, turned a fool,
Giddy with power, or drivelling in his youth,
Would cast his crown and royalties away

To be down-trodden in the mire of streets.
And yet, why not? Doth not this artful Saxon
Hold the great seal of England in his clutches, —
Ride with the king, dice, drink, and dine with him?
Why not, when he who wears the diadem
Of Norman William takes the cast-off wife
Of Louis, king of France, and makes her mistress
Of the same bed where William's holy queen
In travail brought forth princes to this realm?
Why not, when every palace in the kingdom
Haunted by ghosts of his dread predecessors,
When Winchester and Woodstock, Westminster,
Are playhouses, where Circe keeps her court,
As hell or Aquitaine had come to London?

York. Dares the justiciary to mock the king?

Glan. I do not mock the king. Could I but see
This leprosy, which we do call the queen,
Touched by the healing hand of penitence,
My Lord Archbishop, gladly I'd give up
The keys of Henry's treasury and his mace,
Never again to look upon a court.

I love and honor Henry next to God.

YORK. Noble de Glanvil, well I know thou dost;
But who shall now confront him, and rebuke
His wayward love for this same Saxon churl,
And counsel how to fill the vacant see?

GLAN. Go supplicate the queen; she can do much.
You may persuade her to amend her life,
And so perform two offices in one.

YORK. And whither you? This task must not be left
To the poor ministrations of one man.
Besides, it shall be thought I am a rival,
And half my reasons spilled upon the sand.

GLAN. I will bespeak Matilda, the king's mother,
Who scorns the Saxon, and fears not her son.
And then, if it do cost me sword and keys,
Houses and lands, and liberty and life,
I will go with her, meet him face to face,
As he were criminal and I his judge,
And warn him of his madness and its end.

YORK. And I to the queen. Farewell.

[*Exeunt, severally.*

SCENE II. — *Room in palace.*

Enter EMPRESS MATILDA, *mother of* KING HENRY, *and* ELEANOR, *Queen of England.*

MATILDA. Daughter of England, where's your royal lord?

QUEEN. Even now I left him, choleric and pale,
In his own chamber, where he sharply chid me
For bidding him beware the Saxon priest.

MAT. What priest?

QUEEN. Thomas à Becket, madam.

MAT. Archdeacon Becket, Henry's chancellor,
Who, as my Lord of Glanvil hath assured me,
Aspires to be Archbishop of Canterbury?

QUEEN. Ay, the same. I met his grace of York
This very day, and he belabored me
A weary hour with weightiest arguments,
Tending to show the rashness of the step.
He begged me importune his majesty;
And at his instance 'twas that I incurred
So fierce a reprimand.

MAT. 'Tis at request

Of Glanvil I am here to meet the king
Upon this self-same errand.

QUEEN. It is well.
And yet I fear the king will not relent;
His eyes were forkèd lightnings, and his voice
Choked in its utterance, as 'tis wont to do
When strong emotions overmaster him.

MAT. It is the Norman blood that strangles him.
The Conqueror had this grievous malady;
So was my father, the first Henry, cursed.
I fear him not, in madness or in pride;
He is my son in both. Lo! here he comes.

Enter KING HENRY.

KING. Our lady mother, stay you audience?

MAT. Harry of England, I have one request,
My first since you were crowned, perhaps my last.

KING. Make it known boldly, madam. Our decrees
Wait on thee.

MAT. 'Tis spoken gallantly, and like a king,
A Norman king.

KING. Why Norman, madam? I'm of Alfred's blood;
Alfred's, as well as William's. So art thou.
'Twas Alfred gave us laws, maxims, and letters,
Moulded the state into one shapely mass
Wrought out of many jarring dynasties.
Then why not say a Saxon king?

MAT. Nay, Henry, tell me not of Saxon blood!
Me, sprung from their first kings, their mistress born;
Me, whom the churls, forgetful of their oaths
Sworn on the altar where my father crowned me,
Spurned with their feet and bade to stand aside
And give usurping Stephen room to reign:
Me, their victim,
Who fled from Oxford castle in the night,
A dreary winter night, with my four maids,
Our white robes lost amid the whiter snows
That blinded our pursuers while we ran
With freezing feet the long and desolate way
To Abingdon, and thence to Wallingford,

Warmed only by their horses' fiery breath,
As they rode hard behind.

KING. It was the price paid for thy Norman pride.

MAT. I'd pay the same again. I grieve to hear
That England's Henry sorts with Saxon squires,
Gives them his proudest offices of state,
Dines at their tables, quaffs their muddy ale,
And smacks their viands with no kingly relish.

KING. What, is our mother mad?

MAT. With prophecy.
'Tis bruited through the court that you do purpose
To tear the best leaves from our Domesday Book,
To make a new partition of our lands,
And give our Norman castles and high towers
To athelings and thanes, franklins and boors,
To drink your health in till the rafters shake.

KING. They lie who say it.

MAT. Is it then a lie
That Mayor Becket's son, whose Syrian wife
Knew but two words of English when she fled
The land of her nativity, and o'er seas

And continents chased her retreating lover,
Disowned her God, forswore her womanhood —
Is it a lie, that this same swarthy shoot
Of that fierce marriage is to live in state
At Canterbury, and dip his heathen hands
In the pure font that Theobald has blessed?
Is this a lie?

KING. It is no lie, that I do meditate
The elevation of the Chancellor
To the archbishop's see; and it is true
His mother was of Syrian clime and birth.
You do mistake this man.
Jesus was lowly; Peter, James, and John
Were humblest fishermen. The poor, blind world
Knew never yet its teachers while they lived.
It looketh backward o'er a level waste
Worn by the feet of generations gone,
And kens no track save the long-travelled one.
Hence persecutions follow on the footsteps
Of prophets and apostles, seers called,
Because their eyes behold new shapes of truth

Beckoning to paths untrodden by the crowd.
Such is à Becket. Thus his spiritual eye
Sees the far future in the varying instant,
Fathoms the past, and drops a plummet down
To depths before untried. Forgive his birth.
Ask not the mountain from what marshy bed
He lifts his hoary pinnacles to the clouds;
Ask not the clouds, that light the chariot wheels
Of the setting sun with colors mixed in heaven
In what green pool or reptile-haunted fen
Their vapors first were born. Forgive, forgive.
Peace, love, and charity are lowly bred.

Enter ARCHBISHOP OF YORK *and* GLANVIL.

But in happy time
Here come good counsellors. Welcome, my Lord of York!
And you, Lord Glanvil, you are welcome, too.
When came your grace from York?

YORK. Since morning, sire. How fares your majesty?

KING. Well, and yet ill.

MAT. My Lord Archbishop, he is well in health,
But, like myself, o'erwearied and distraught
With such perplexities as men like you
Can best resolve.

YORK. And what are they, your highness?

KING. I am berated by two mighty queens
Upon a great affair of state.

QUEEN. My lord,
Not two. I cry you mercy. I am dumb.

KING. 'Tis well that women should be listeners;
But silence never was a practised art
Among the ladies of a Norman court.

MAT. Else merry England had been Saxon still.

YORK. What is the subject of this grave dispute?

QUEEN. If Becket shall be made archbishop or no.

YORK. Of Canterbury? God in heaven forbid!

MAT. Amen!

KING. Most suddenly dispatched, and most devoutly.
Will you vouchsafe a reason, my good lord?

YORK. His life is scathed with fierce, unhallowed
fires;
He hath been lewd and wanton in his youth,
Headstrong in manhood, hot and passionate.
Besides, he comes not of the noble line
Your predecessors honored with that see.
I do beseech your majesty, forbear
To put so great affront upon the realm,
Such mockery on the old nobility,
Such sharp indignity upon myself.

KING. What, would'st thou add this see to that of
York?
England would then scarce need a king at all.

YORK. My liege, you ask for reasons but to spurn
them.
I will give no more.

KING. [*Angrily.*] I asked for reasons, not conceits,
my lord.
Lord Glanvil, thou art wise and sound of heart;
Answer, shall Becket have the vacant see?

GLAN. My lord,

It irks me not what blood may course the veins
Of any priest or prelate, if his soul
Be but besprinkled with redeeming drops
And his hands spotless from the stains of earth.
Becket is chancellor;
He hath the seal of England. It is well.
And there, by my advice,
Your gracious bounty should repose itself.
But if you do advance this restless man —
Rash, wilful, hard, fiery, and turbulent—
Into the porches of that holy fane,
Repentance yet shall drive your grace to kneel
At its high altar, sorrowing for the act.

MAT. And still I say, amen!

QUEEN. And I!

YORK. And I!

KING. Hark you, my mistresses, and echoing lords,
I do suspect ye of conspiracy.
Am I your dupe and tool? Your minion I,
Practised upon, and made the target's eye,
Whereat your well-concerted shafts are levelled?

But they shall glance aside from England's shield.
You, madam, [*To Matilda,*]
As this our island is too small
To hold us twain, get you to Normandy;
I do appoint you regent of that duchy.
There dominate to your proud heart's content.
For you, my lady queen, the masquers wait.
Lords York and Glanvil, you are grave, good men,
With weighty avocations. Leave me all.

Exeunt MATILDA, ELEANOR, YORK, *and* GLANVIL.

KING. Go, summon to the presence instantly
The chancellor.
[*Exit attendant.*
The ministers and prelates of the kingdom,
The barons and the petty officers,
Are leagùed all to thwart my purposes.
By the Conqueror's bones!
This Saxon-Syrian shall have the see,
If its proud mitre scorch his shrinking brows,
Its crozier blight his hand with leprosy!

Enter BECKET.

BECKET. Did the king summon me?

KING. We did; on business of high import.

BECKET. How can I serve your majesty?

KING. By stepping nearer to the throne.

BECKET. The halo of the sceptre even now
Dazzles my eyes. Methinks I am too near.

KING. We will contract the pupils of thine eyes,
Till they, like eagles, look upon the sun.

BECKET. What means your highness?

KING. To be blunt,
I have bethought me long to fill the see
Left vacant by the primate Theobald;
And, after pondering now these eighteen months,
Revolving in my mind some dozen prelates
Who seem too light for such a load of care,
I have resolved to proffer it to thee.

BECKET. My sovereign lord, the weary weight would crush me.
Already do I groan beneath your bounty.
The offices of chancellor were much;

Besides, I am provost of Beverly,
The dean of Hastings, constable of the Tower;
The baronies of Eye and Berkham, too,
Rest in my keeping; and the young prince Henry,
Presumptive heir of England, is my pupil,
And looks to me to mirror to his eyes
The graces of a king.
Yet more, my life hath flaws
That shrewd, inspecting men, with biting tongues,
Would fail not to make patent to the world.
Again, I never led a hermit's life,
Nor shaved my head, nor sandalled yet my feet,
To go upon a saintly pilgrimage,
Nor felt the damp of cloisters, nor did penance,
Nor won the favors of suffragan bishops,
Who, for such elevation, needs must hate me.
My culture is in letters, knightly feats,
Gaming and hunting, hawking, horsemanship.
I have fought battles, too, and shed men's blood,
At Toulouse, as your majesty doth know,
And on the borders of fair Normandy,

Where, at my cost, I kept twelve hundred knights.
I lack the holy unction of a life
Spent in meek charities and lowly duties,
Savoring of sanctity. My heart is proud;
My ear is tickled with the applause of scholars,
And my eye bends to the nodding of a plume.
I love the war-cry of Plantagenet
Better than anthems piercing gothic roofs,
And the long wailing of a bugle note
Touches me more than silvery bells at vespers.
The laugh of peasant girls, proud ladies' smiles,
Are dearer to me than the sighs of nuns,
Whose hearts keep time to ebon rosaries.
Pardon me, sire, I *dare* not take the see.

KING. Have I not been your friend in darkest hours,
Championed your weakness, gloried in your strength,
And stood your brother rather than your master?
And will you now deny me the poor favor
Of taking greatness, when I stoop with it
As bedesmen do when they would ask an alms?

BECKET. [*Kneeling.*] Your lowliest abject, on my knees I beg
Your majesty take from my weary back
The load that else will bow me to the earth.

KING. Becket, dost thou refuse the see?

BECKET. I only supplicate. Refuse I may not,
Though to accept it break a loyal heart.
For well I know the gift in hands like mine,
Sharp as a sword, forever from me severs
The ties of friendship 'twixt my king and me.

KING. That risk be mine. When wilt thou be invested?

BECKET. A brave man, once condemned to death,
Asks not an hour's reprieve. Even when thou wilt.

KING. Rise from thy knees. Put on a smiling face.
Thou shalt crown kings and sit with pontiffs.

BECKET. I shall sit alone
In sackcloth and in humbleness. Farewell.

[*Exit.*

KING. I like it not. Why did he say "farewell"?
His voice was hollow as a sepulchre,

And his dark eye, though swimming in its tears,
Looked forth a stern adieu. I like it not.
Was it from sorrow, or a deep resolve?
And Glanvil's warning! And Matilda's, too!
Shall I go call him back? No, no, I'll trust him.

[*Exit.*

SCENE III. — *Palace at Woodstock.*

Enter QUEEN, *agitated.*

QUEEN. My worst fears ar econfirmed. I am a victim
To this incontinent and treacherous king.
Proofs multiply — duped, fooled, and cheated;
But I will be revenged! (*Weeps passionately.*)

Enter MATILDA.

MAT. What means this violent grief?

QUEEN. Would I were dead!
I loathe this gloomy Woodstock and its park;
Its oaks and mistletoes, its fogs and rains,
Its owls and rooks;
I hate the very tones
Of its dull clock, telling from yonder tower
The watches of the night.

MAT. This is no cause
For passionate weeping. Some deep-seated sorrow
Preys on your heart.

QUEEN. Even so. An agony
Burning and torturing, that I dare not whisper
In any ear, — least of all, in a mother's.

MAT. Ha! Henry is the cause. Again I charge you
Tell me the secret of this keen distress.

QUEEN. You will take part against me. You will never
Believe the thing that shames you.

MAT. I will know
The truth, — credit and vindicate the truth.
Lady, dry up these bitter tears, and tell me
Speedily what hath chanced.

QUEEN. Have you not heard
Rumors touching the marriage of the king,
Ere my divorce from Louis, king of France,
With Rosamond, the daughter of Lord Clifford?
That I am but a mistress to his lusts,
And my sons not legitimate?

MAT. Yes, daughter;
I have heard it gossiped through the court,
Questioned the king, who, with a solemn oath,
Denies it. I believe him.

QUEEN. I believe
Nothing but my own eyes and ears. I have
Proofs, madam.

MAT. Unfold them to me.

QUEEN. To solve
This mystery, I stole into the park,
An hour ago, and hid behind a pollard,
Near which so often I had seen him pass.
Not long I waited, when my stealthy lord,
Emerging from a thicket, sauntered by
So near I heard his breath. A thread of silk,
Knotting its coils around one glittering spur,
Rustled among the leaves and trailed behind.
Breathless, I darted forth all unperceived,
Following the doublings of this treacherous clue,
Until I traced it to a tuft of brambles,
That shaded the park wall, and there espied

This tell-tale ball of floss; and, glancing through
The thorny screen, lo, a small, secret gate
Led to a winding passage underground.
There, thrilling the dark labyrinth, I heard
A warbled strain with tinkling lute-notes mixed.
It was a woman's voice. What say you, madam,
Are my suspicions idle?

MAT. This proves nothing.
A humming-bird in honeysuckle bower,
Fluttering amongst the vines, — a willing mistress
Unto a liberal master. 'Tis the blur,
The blot of our whole line of kings. But this
Taints not your issue, cannot shake their rights
To the succession.

QUEEN. This, too, he denies.
Being false in this, how can I trust his word
In that?

MAT. One is a common vice; the other
A crime and villainy affecting knighthood.
I'll not believe it.

QUEEN. I will be resolved.

If it prove true, I'll set the world ablaze.
I could forgive this treachery to me,
But to my children — never!

MAT. Trust me, daughter,
You are deceived.

QUEEN. I am wronged.

MAT. Be patient —
Be secret — watch the king — I will watch, too.
Ours is a common cause; for Henry's honor
Is mine — your children are my grandsons.
I will look to it. [*Exit.*

QUEEN. Ha, my pretty warbler,
These silken gyves shall thread your little feet,
And still the fluttering of your wanton wings;
And yonder brambles shall be twigs of lime,
To moult your feathers while they tear your skin;
And I will turn your song to such a wail
Your very fledglings shall forsake the nest.
My children, — oh, my children!

[*Exit.*

Scene IV.

Audience chamber in the palace of the Archbishop of Canterbury. *Time—evening. Enter* Archbishop.

It is as I foreboded; I was made
Archbishop but to pander to the greed
Of Henry, and despoil God's treasure-house
To cram the royal vaults at Winchester
With jewels from our holy shrines and altars.
It shall not be; these hands are consecrate
To holy offices; this brow marked with the sign
That kings can ne'er erase.

Enter Philip, *the Pope's legate.* Archbishop *extends his hand*

How fares the ambassador of his holiness?
I fear me our poor house of Canterbury
Yields meagre entertainment to such guest.

Philip. 'Tis princely, my lord Archbishop.

Arch. 'Tis thine own.
I craved thine audience here to solve a doubt.

Philip. What my poor counsels can, I freely give.

Arch. There is a tempest gathering in the heavens;
Bolts cleave the vault, and rumbling, distant thunders

Begin to shake the rock-ribbed isle ; the king,
Seizing the occasion of divided rule
Between two claimants for the papal see,
Hath placed me here to rifle and to rend
The church, not keep it. Tell me, dost thou think
Pope Alexander dare outface the monarch
And give countenance to me?

PHILIP. He dare ; he will.
What has your grace to fear? Your palace gates
Are thronged with princes and ambassadors;
Dukes kneel to you, and haughty earls are waiting,
Like humble squires, to crave your benison.
Largess flows in as rivers seek the sea,
And the best revenues of the kingdom lie
Crouched at your feet to swell your lordly state.
'Tis true, the hosts are mustering to the battle ;
But sceptres crumble when they touch the robes
Of sanctity like yours. Be calm, and brave the storm.

ARCH. Why, so I will. But little canst thou know
The strength of the Plantagenet, his pride,
His avarice, and the fury of his rage.

He loved me once; and natures such as his,
When once they change from love to hate, become
Like lava from a mountain's feverish lips.

PHILIP. Are you not still
Lord chancellor? That you are left to enjoy
Such marks of confidence, methinks, is much.

ARCH. I have resigned it; notified the king
That henceforth God alone shall be my master;
That I am England's primate and not his.

Enter monk, who stands at a distance.

What ails thee, son? Approach; what said the king?
Did he accept my resignation?

MONK. No,
My lord, he threw the letters back and bade
You burn them and the hand that writ them.

ARCH. Well?

MONK. And sent me hurrying home to tell your grace
To meet him within three days at Winchester.
Called thee — I know not what.

ARCH. [*To Philip.*] Dost hear the news?
To Winchester? I go to Winchester?
The primate's seat, methought, was Canterbury.
The chancellor may to Winchester; I'll stay
At Canterbury.

PHILIP. God keep thee firm.

ARCH. Nay, more. God give me courage.
Firmness is passive, and but keeps her own;
But I must act, and action calls for courage.
Thus with my staff,
Like the old Roman, I strike off the heads
Of the tallest poppies first.
[*To monk.*] Go, forthwith, summon to our court, Earl
Clare;
Cite him to render up the barony
Of Tunbridge, which the conqueror William reft
From this our see of Canterbury and bestowed
Upon Clare's ancestors, against the rules
And canons of the church.

Taking a sealed package from his bosom, delivers it to him.

This paper gives thee cure of Westerly,
A manor held by William de Eynsford,
Under earl Clare,
Who claims the right of presentation
From the crown. The right is ours; was plucked
By usurpation from us. I bestow
The living upon thee. Abuse it not.
And hark ye! Lest the fellow may resist,
I'll send an escort to instate thee there
Of twenty valorous knights.
I never sought the primacy; but now,
Since I am primate made against my wish,
There's not a tithe of cummin or of mint,
No old observance, custom, reverence,
Nor pomp of form, nor shadow of respect,
Shall be abated from our mother church.
The king's prerogative shall be taught to keep
Its ancient limits; and its haughty waves,
Foaming, shall dash against opposing rocks.

ACT II.

SCENE I. — *Palace at Winchester. Enter* GLANVIL *and gentlemen of King's household.*

GLAN. Welcome, my lord of Leicester and lord Cornwall!
I hear his majesty hath sent for you.
The times are very boisterous, and he seeks
Your sagest counsels.

LEICES. The Arch-prelate Becket
Threatens strange innovations in the state.

CORN. 'Tis said he reaches forth to pluck the crown.

GLAN. Two popes in Europe — Becket, pope of England.
Where will it end?

CORN. Hath the king yet returned from Woodstock?

GLAN. But an hour ago. Lo! where he comes!

[*Enter* KING.

KING. (*Angrily.*) Resign the chancellorship, forsooth!
And charge me with encroaching on the rights

And dues of holy Mother Church; usurping
Her demesnes, her benefices, gold;
And gorging her thin livings to bloat up
My overgrown prerogatives!
The man is mad. I'll have him chained and dungeoned.
My lords,
We cry you mercy! Ye are very welcome.
Since Becket's coronation, our poor house
Shows like a hermitage; yet are ye welcome.

CORN. All travel-stained we come,
Seeking to show our duty in our haste,
And our obeisance by our soiled neglect.

KING. My gentle lords, your presence like the sun
Sucks up the damps and vapors of the night.
And Glanvil, too! Lord Glanvil, pardon me!
I am your debtor for a store of patience.
My temper is too splenetic. Alack!
It is a humor in our Norman veins,
That taints the race; it is the Viking blood
Churned into foam by tossing of our keels

Upon the British and the German seas.
Look you, I was in fault; and better 'tis
I should confess it than that thou shouldst grieve.
Here is my hand. I did mistake that man.
Methought some drops of gratitude did warm
His heart. My bread he broke and drank my wine;
Lived in the very shadow of the throne;
I trusted him and loved him as myself,
But the thawed serpent stung me.

GLAN. (*Deeply moved.*) Oh, my liege!

KING. Not a word more. Now being in the net,
Why — we must gnaw the meshes and get free.

[*Enter* EARL CLARE.

Now had I been to choose, there's not a man
In England better welcome than earl Clare.

CLARE. My liege, are title deeds and old prescriptions
Still binding in this realm?

KING. Well may you ask!
But why this angry haste?

CLARE. The first earl Clare, a century ago,
When with the Conqueror he crossed the channel,

Had granted to himself and heirs, in fee,
The barony of Tunbridge.

KING. 'Twas his due.
Long may his goodly line enjoy the gift;
And cursed be he that seeks to wrest it from them.

CLARE. Thou dost curse England's primate.
Becket hath robbed me of it.

KING. He dare not do it! Tunbridge?

CLARE. It is done.

KING. Upon what plea?

CLARE. That it belonged to Canterbury.

KING. Why, then, do Winchester, Woodstock, the Tower,
Westminster, the crown, the Thames, and London
Belong to Becket. By the Conqueror's bones!
I'll choke the priest till he do vomit up
This morsel!

CLARE. Was I not tenant *in capite* of the manor
Of Westerly, with right of presentation?

KING. Thou wert and art.

CLARE. Becket

Hath thrust my curate out with violent hands
And placed a canting friar in his room.

KING. Turn him out and cut his throat!

CLARE. Why, so I did; which when the archbishop heard,
He straightway excommunicated me.

KING. Thou'rt mad. He could not excommunicate
A tenant of the crown, unauthorized.

CLARE. Yet he hath done it. Look, his signature!

[*Shows a paper.*

KING. The incorrigible knave! Go to him straight
And in my name command him to absolve thee.
What, is the law of England abrogate
And every ancient title turned adrift
To be dog-eared and slimed by slippery priests?
What shall be done, my lord justiciary?

GLAN. By my advice, a council should be called
Of all the barons and prelates in the kingdom,
To ratify anew our ancient laws,
And fix the boundaries of prerogative
Betwixt the church and state.

KING. 'Tis well advised.
What say the earls of Leicester, Cornwall, Clare?
ALL. 'Tis well.
KING. My gentle lords, I thank you all.
These constitutions, drawn with nicest care,
Shall be the barrier where opposing tides
May meet and dash in harmless violence.
God be my witness, not the meanest churl
That tills our English soil by our consent
Shall stand in his degree to any law
Amenable more than our crownéd self,
Primate or bishop, duke or belted earl;
But each, in order, garnishing the state
From its firm base to its heaven-kissing towers,
Shall in the fabric fill his wonted place.
Be this the basis of the British law;
And on these constitutions be upreared,
Age after age, the temple of our rule.
We will send out our heralds instantly.
Meet we at Clarendon all our estates.
Summon the primate thither with the rest

To answer there ; and bid the legate Philip
Carry the parchment to pope Alexander,
And tell him, if 'tis ratified, our sword
Shall be thrown in the scale 'gainst Pascal third,
And Europe own henceforth one pontiff's sway
From sea to sea.

SCENE II. — *Room in a cottage in the park at Woodstock.*

TIME — *Evening.*

ROSAMOND CLIFFORD *seated near a window at her embroidery.*

ROSAMOND. The hours drag on; the clock from yonder tower,
In telling them, is less alone than I.
The oaks stand dim against the sky as spectres.
Oh, the weary sighs,
The watchings, doubts, and fears of this long night!
Before that dismal coronation day
Plantagenet would scarcely leave my side,
But hung about the cottage day and night;
Read, sung to me, and frolicked with my boys;
Called William, Long Sword, Geoffrey, the Lord Bishop;

Said I should be his queen when he was crowned,
As, long ago, I was his wedded wife.
And by his halidom swore oft and oft,
My forehead would set off a diadem
Better than when it wore a bridal chaplet.
But now he comes not oft and briefly tarries;
Smiles seldom, and even his kisses seem to chide;
And never whispers he of royalty.
Something's awry, that Henry hides from me.
Hark, where he comes!

[*Enter* KING HENRY.

KING. My Rosamond!

ROSA. My husband, lover, king! [*They embrace.*
Why stay so late, till every star gets pale
With watching for thy coming?

KING. Yet one star
Lingers still ruddy, filling all my heaven
With diamond-pointed beams.

ROSA. Ah, flatterer!
But why so late? No subterfuge, no shift,
No subtle make-believe. Say, why so late?

KING. How fares the Long-Sword?

ROSA. But say, why so late?

KING. And how my little Bishop?

ROSA. Nay, why so late?

KING. Business of state, my love; an audience
Of half a dozen prelates and ten earls,
And every minister about the court.
Even as it was, with most unkingly haste
I did dismiss them, and have spurred my horse
To a swift gallop with no breath of pause
From Westminster to Woodstock.

ROSA. Is that sooth?

KING. Ay, by the rood!

ROSA. Upon your knightly word?
Your honor, spurs, and Christian manhood?

KING. Yes.

ROSA. So then I answer that your sons are well.
William grows taller half a head a day;
Geoffrey's dark, loving eyes, deep as a well,
Though shaded more and more by their brown lashes,
Let in sun-glimpses of a quiet joy.

O husband, lord, great king and god on earth
To thy poor wife and blessed, beauteous boys,
When shall we know the sweets that once we tasted,
When, sitting on this floor, you romped with them
As lightly as the keeper of your game
In yonder park; while I stood happy by
And clapped my hands in gleeful ecstasy!
Oh! couldst thou know what sorrow absence brings;
How my poor eyes throb, how my fingers tremble,
My thoughts far absent from my needle-work,
Shaping bright pictures upon palace walls,
Then wouldst thou pity me!

KING. Sweet Rosamond, you stab me to the heart.

ROSA. [*Weeping and clinging to him.*]
On battle-field
Can you not dub a valiant squire a knight,
Create an earl a duke? And who dare frown
Or look upon you with a jaundiced eye,
If you shall own me queen, your children princes?

KING. But stay a little, till the fitting hour,
Till rebel trumpets bray not in my kingdom.

Tarry till Normandy is put to rest,
And then thou shalt be crowned.

ROSA. Plantagenet,
Still will I tarry — hope — believe.

KING. And win.

SCENE III. — *Palace at Westminster.*

Enter ARCHBISHOP OF YORK *and* GLANVIL.

YORK. 'Tis said that our pope-primate signed at last
The constitutions.

GLAN. Doubting, hesitating,
With now a backward, now a forward step,
I hear he did. Now lifting high in air
His dignities prelatical, and now
Low trailing them in the dust; now shuddering
At the dread mention of pope Alexander, —
Asking the messengers with ashen lips
And choking utterance if all the bishops
Had signed the constitutions willingly,
Or from constraint.

YORK. Traitor and hypocrite!

GLAN. Enthusiast rather; lifted up so high

Above the marshy level of his birth,
That his brain reels like oaks on mountain ledges
When lightnings splinter them. A bigot wild,
Drunk with the ecstasy of some conceit,
Or tempting intimations of some fiend,
Who, habiting his dark and nether sphere,
Waves an invisible hand to this poor slave,
Who kneels or rises, prays or prophesies
At bidding of his master. Such is Becket.

York. More villain he than victim, by my thought.

Glan. Through long experience in the civil courts,
Oft have I seen such random-thoughted men
Wrapped in the cloudy mantle of their dreams;
Men that loved night and sorrow, sought lone dells;
Housed them in caverns, questioned grisly shadows,
Talked with familiars, rolled their haggard eyes
At substances so thin, that other men
Saw nothing save the all-surrounding air.
I've heard them talk of doom, and backward start
At call of trumpet, or the cry of souls
Shut up in horrible hells. Such man is Becket,

Or I'm at fault. No hypocrite, my lord.

[*Enter* KING HENRY.

KING. What lunatic fool dost thou discourse of, Glanvil?
We'll give him to the sanitary keeping
Of our late chancellor.

GLAN. It was of him we spake. His grace of York
Holds him a villain; I for one possessed.

KING. Villain in heart and of disordered head;
The sum of both your moieties sums him up.
Rebel is his addition.

YORK. Why not imprison Becket?

KING. The pope — The pope —

YORK. Let me first be pope's legate, and then act.

KING. Yet something must we do
Even on the instant.

YORK. Why not pursue him then
With charges that shall strip from off his back
The garb of sanctity that awes the rabble?
Was he not long in office? Might he not
Appropriate to his own use the funds

He held in trust for others?

KING. Ay, my lord.

His lavish life, the splendor of his house,
His state, his equipages and his pride
While late in office, countenance such a charge.
What say'st thou, Glanvil?

GLAN. Boldly may I speak?

KING. Boldly and to the point.

GLAN. My liege, I have
Two beings, an outer and an inner life.
One is made up of hard and crusty facts,
Of circumstances, shifts, and policies.
The other is a silent consciousness,
That, like to water darkened under ice,
Or flowers or green grass hid by rustling leaves,
Though all unseen, its still vitality
Forever keepeth in my secret soul.
This last I trust to with a trembling hope,
Leaving the seen for the invisible.
Its promptings following will I do no wrong,
Nor counsel evil that a good may come.

Wherefore say I, accuse not this hot primate
With crimes, which either he hath not committed
Or which are pardoned by thy long delays.
For trust me, natures, such as his, best thrive
By persecutions, covet buffetings,
And least they suffer when they suffer most.
It shall be said the king hath wronged the man ;
Factions shall gather round the controversy,
Feuds shall arise, and scandals get abroach ;
Women shall whisper, boys shall prattle it,
And the cross-grained and wolfish multitude
Shall feast their eyes upon his sorry visage,
His hair shirt, and his sackcloth, and his tears,
And cry, " There goes the martyr, the good Becket,
Whose faults were holiness and honesty."

KING. Thus ever spinning fine and subtle threads,
Thy gauzy web, intangible as ether,
Not palpable to sense or common reason,
Floats round thee like a veil. My lord of York,
Shall the promoters have this priest in charge ?

YORK. By my advice they shall.

KING. It shall be done.

GLAN. My hands are clean.

KING. The blood be on our head.
My lords, this is a boding and distempered time;
The church, that once did feed our hungry souls,
Now snatches from our mouth the wholesome bread,
That in the midst of plenty we do starve.
For her, our navies wing the ridgy deep,
And like a river, swollen beyond its banks,
She desolates the fair face of our valleys
With channels huge and islands of ribbed sand.
Murders are done by priests in holy vestments;
Robberies, adulteries, fornications, rapes,
And thefts and simonies defy the law,
Subjected but to spiritual ban.

Enter PHILIP, *pope's legate.*

What, art thou winged, and dost thou fly from France?
For sure, no wind could waft thee with such speed.
What said his holiness to our constitutions?

PHIL. He conned them o'er and o'er, and line by line,
And with grave care pondered each article;
Spent a whole night in solemn meditation —
Deliberated — prayed — and then —

KING. Ratified?

PHIL. In part — yes, as thou sayest — ratified —

KING. In part, forsooth! Why not the whole — all — all?
How many was he pleased to ratify?

PHIL. Six articles. [*Hands paper to king.*]

KING. [*Taking paper and examining it.*]
From sixteen, only six?
What right had he with apostolic shears
To slit his ear-marks in our edicts thus;
Pocket the text, and send the crumpled margin
Scrawled with interpolations, commentaries,
And blundering friar's Latin, back to us,
Bloated with phrases gouty as his thumb;
Stuffed out with expletives that nod their heads
Like a whole college of ecclesiastics

When they have dined? These reeling periods,
Not german to the matter of our thoughts,
More than our island to the estuaries
Where muddy Tiber and the lazy sea
Meet in a brackish marsh — we'll none of them!
Six articles — from sixteen only six —
Say — why not blot them all? From sixteen — six!
And they so idle, insignificant,
That I had thought to cancel every one,
And send the other ten! What, did he pray —
And meditate — and read — and waste the night,
To throw away ten kernels and then cull
Six baggage husks, fit only for the swine?
Hark thee, sir legate! there's another pope!
We have not yet declared between them twain.
Upon my conscience I have grievous doubts,
And I must go alone — kneel — pray for light —
Con — spell — burn incense and deliberate,
Which of the two I'll ratify, and he —
He shall be pope of Christendom! Six devils!

SCENE IV. — *An oratory in the* ARCHBISHOP OF CANTERBURY'S *palace. The archbishop, clothed in sackcloth, stands looking at a crucifix that is placed in a niche in the wall.*

ARCH. "Foxes have holes and birds of the air
have nests."
Thus saidst thou, suffering God, in Bethlehem,
Beyond the Jordan's bounds, on Olivet,
Wandering through wheat fields, vineyards, olive
yards,
Tossed by the billows of Genesareth,
The dews of night falling upon thy temples
And standing in cold drops upon thy hair;
For thee the barren fig-tree bore no fruit,
And David's city, with its palaces,
Its haughty priests and sacrificial smoke,
No shelter gave. While I, a perjured wretch,
My broken vows still warm upon my lips,
Am housed and fed with more than Pilate's pomp.
Fasting henceforth, I will endure the cold,
Dress me in rags and wash the feet of beggars,

Discharge no functions of my sacred office,
Till thou and thy vicegerent do absolve me.

[*Enter* BISHOP OF WINCHESTER.

WIN. How fares your grace?

ARCH. I am lost! alas,
I have invoked the curse, and it is on me.
My hand upon my mouth, my mouth in the dust,
Give not one answering sign.

WIN. What hast thou done?

ARCH. For a king's favor sold the church of God!
Alas! alas! would that the hated pen,
With which I set my execrated name
To that vile parchment, had consumed my hand!
Would that cursed name were blotted from the earth!

WIN. Why, look! thou art absolved! Philip, the legate —

ARCH. What, hath he returned?

WIN. He hath.

ARCH. What news?

WIN. The pope hath ratified six articles,
The rest rejected; the besotted king

Hath thrown his gauntlet down in terrible wrath.
The pope hath need of thee. Thou art absolved.

ARCH. Then God be praised! Now for the bitter strife.

WIN. 'Tis time for action.
Hast thou not heard that all thy personal goods
Are confiscate to the king — that thou art fined
For non-appearance in the civil court?

ARCH. For non-appearance, when I sent a knight
To implead me there?

WIN. The bishops all,
Save Folliot of London, gave thee bail,
Which but the more enraged the furious king.

ARCH. I thank their love, and yet I need it not.
This touches not the church; this is mine own.
Why, let the king rob me; viewed as a man,
What's Becket but a subject? 'Twas a wrong;
But other men have wrongs. Let him rob Becket,
Turn him out of doors, or in the Tower
Lodge him with clanking chains about his wrists,

Becket shall say amen; if he'll have Becket's
lands,
His ambling palfrey, or his hawk or hounds,
Why, let him take them — this is personal.
But mark you! the archbishop of Canterbury,
In all that's functional to his high office,
Will quit no doit of his prerogative,
Nor rend a feather from its spreading wings.

Enter JOHN, *Mareschal of the Exchequer.*

MAR. My lord, your grace is cited to appear
In the exchequer court, to answer straight
Some certain accusations there preferred,
Touching your character as chancellor.

ARCH. And who the accuser?

MAR. The king, please your grace.

ARCH. What am I charged withal?

MAR. Squandering the moneys
Received in trust, appropriating them
To your own use.

ARCH. What sums? What moneys?

MAR. The revenues of baronies and abbeys,
Of prelacies and other several trusts
Committed to your care.

ARCH. When must I answer?

MAR. To-morrow.

ARCH. Leave me. I will consider of it.
To-morrow render him a full recital [*Exit Mareschal.*
Of all the doings of that long, long term —
Cast my accounts — gather my vouchers up
From mouldy chests and vaults in one short day —
Present — explain them? 'Tis impossible!
O Winchester, this is too fell a blow.
My property and private rights I gave
As freely as my master took them from me.
When summoned, I disdained to plead for them.
My public character is not mine own,
It is the nation's — God's. Stand by the sea
When the winds chafe it, and note well its waters —
How they do take the colors of the shore;
Here stained with earth, there glassing on their bosom
Dark forms of trees, brown knolls, and slanting hills,

Or the pale glimmer of some flinty cliff;
While far away, lo! leaping to the light,
Pure, jubilant, with heaven's own hues upon them,
They stretch forever. Such my checkered life.
When near its margin stained, — shaded with sin;
Tinged with the grain of all vicissitudes,
With vices flecked, irregularities;
But, in its bolder depths, where navies rode
And lone birds flew, stars slept, and sunbeams shimmered,
In all its wide circumference, no blot,
No cloud; no widows wronged, no orphan's bread,
Snatched from his hungry lips, no barony
Limping upon its crutches from a wound
I gave it, and no charity turned thwart
To run in channels dug not by its founders.
My character official I'll protect.
Thrice hath this mad king cited me to court;
As often have I set my rights adrift
To dash in pieces upon treacherous rocks.
Now will I meet him with a steady eye,

And he shall quail before it as the viper
Shrinks from the fire.

SCENE V. — *Palace at Woodstock — Enter* QUEEN.

QUEEN. Walls cannot hide the secret! Here's the key!
Within this very hour I will know all!
Would I could meet the monarch and his mate
In one another's arms!

[*Enter* BECKET.

BECKET. Madam, a word.
Tell me, what means this wild and ruffled air,
Those bloodshot eyes, clenched hands, that tottering step?

QUEEN. Methought I was alone.

BECKET. You are alone, my Lady.
I am a solitude upon whose ear
A whispered word may fall without an echo.
Looking into your eyes, I know your thoughts, —
I feel your pulses quickening in my heart;
You hate me, and I come to save you, madam.
The very Saxon blood that you have scorned,

Thrills with your sorrows, kindles at your wrongs.

QUEEN. My lord?

ARCH. Hanging above your head, behold
Loose rocks ready to drop and crush you.

QUEEN. [*Rushing toward him and seizing his hand.*]
Father!
Tell me, let me know all — the worst — have mercy —
Take pity —

BECKET. How then if you betray me?
Wise men lock up their hearts and keep the key;
Fools give it to the keeping of their foes.

QUEEN. I was deceived — cajoled by lying tongues
To trust evil reports; and learned too late
That truth and honor, like the sweetest flowers,
Oft grow in wildest soil, upspringing free,
Nursed only by the sunshine and the dew.
Pardon me, trust me, save me!

ARCH. 'Twas my errand.
You are a victim of conspiracy;
You bear the name; another has the right;
You are a shadow. This is my surmise,

Vouched by slight instances; such mites and straws
As gusty rumor whirled about my ears
When he, who calls you wife, could call me friend.
He calls her wife, too.

QUEEN. Tell me her name!

ARCH. [*Pointing to the key.*]
You have the wand; touch but the siren's lips,
They will reveal the secret.

QUEEN. I will unseal her lips, then lock them up
In everlasting winter!

ARCH. That is death!

QUEEN. Death and the hell that follows it!

ARCH. No!

QUEEN. Yes!
Death — torturing, lingering, horrible death.

ARCH. No bloodshed! I will have no blood upon
Your hands or my white vestments.

QUEEN. I will steep
My lips in blood, — her blood!

ARCH. [*Going.*] Madam, farewell.

QUEEN. Stay, father! I am weak, blind, desolate!

Lend me your counsels! I will follow them,
Lead to what gulf they will!

ARCH. They shall lead up
To light. Now listen! Go explore yon cavern
Of secrecy and shame. Search its dark vaults,
Flash on its guilty gems those kindling eyes.
Henry, your eldest son, shall fly to France
And stir up Louis to espouse your cause;
Gain his consent, his daughter Marguerite,
Henry's affianced, shall be forthwith crowned
With the young prince at Westminster. Let Richard
Haste to Poitou, where he shall find the nobles
Ripe for revolt. Young Henry shall be crowned —

QUEEN. You too are wronged!
His grace of York hath new canonicals
To inaugurate the functions of a primate
As new as they.

ARCH. Madam, Roger of York
Shall never crown the prince.

QUEEN. Heaven grant he may not!

ARCH. I say he shall not! All the precedents

Devolve this right on me.

QUEEN. The king will make
New precedents.

ARCH. I will annul them then.
But to thy search.

QUEEN. Father, I go. Farewell.

[*She unlocks the door and disappears.*

ARCH. I, Becket, primate by the grace of God,
Will pour the sacred oil on Henry's head;
Else shall the throne be vacant, and the crown
Grow pale among the stars of Christendom.

[*Exit.*

ACT III.

SCENE I.—*A room in* ROSAMOND'S *cottage.* ROSAMOND *takes up her lute and sings.*

The ivy hides the rifted tower,
  The mosses gray and old,
Nor minds the wind, nor heeds the shower,
  Nor shrinks from winter's cold;
The daisy laughs upon the lea
  Through all the dew-damp night,

And looks the sunbeams in the face
  With eyes of cheerful light.
Both love the open air, the sky,
  And both imprisoned droop and die.

Oh, let me be the ivy, free
  To vault and climb at will,
Or daisy with bright eye to see
  The sun rise from the hill.
Unbolt the doors; throw wide the gates,
  And let my feverish lip
Grow ruddy in the frolic gales,
  The bubbling fountains sip.
Like the wild forest and the sea
  Let my heart throb with liberty.

While she is singing, QUEEN ELEANOR *enters unperceived, and stands looking at her until the song is concluded.*

QUEEN. [*Advancing.*] What, pine to break the bars of such a cage?

ROSA. Madam, who are you?

QUEEN. The minion's pert! Hark ye!
I have no time for archery of words.
Such sports become the king; my humor is

To know what keeps so gay a butterfly
Absent so long from sunshine and from flowers.
When didst thou see thy royal lover last ?
A dainty lip to smother with a kiss.
Were I a king,
I might be tempted to a forest glade
A many nights to look on such a nymph.
When didst thou see thy royal lover last ?

ROSA. Thou dost insult me, madam. Leave the cottage.

QUEEN. Passion shows like an angel in thee. Come,
Pretty penitent, 'tis time for shrift ; confess
All thy relations to this gallant monarch ;
How oft he comes, how late he lingers here ;
How many pledges hast thou of his love ;
What he hath promised that he not performs ;
The hopes and fears that flutter in thy heart.
Confess ! confess !

ROSA. Who art thou ?

QUEEN. The Queen !

ROSA. The Queen? Whose Queen?

QUEEN. Henry Plantagenet's.

ROSA. Proud woman, it is false. I am the queen,—
The mate of Henry, long and dearly loved;
The mother of his sons, wife of his youth,
His, ere the king of Scotland dubbed him knight;
His, ere he fleshed his sword in any field;
His, by the holy vow, the golden ring,
By a pure bosom and a faith unstained.
Unhappy woman, thou art much abused;
And, God forgive him, he is much to blame,
To stain that lily forehead with his lust,
To spot that white breast with his treacheries,
And soil that tender hand with the rash touch
Of passion all unblessed.
He is to blame — to blame! I am ashamed
That I did speak ungentle words to thee.

While Rosamond is speaking, Eleonor stands looking fixedly at her.

QUEEN. What vouchers hast thou that thou art his wife?

ROSA. This diamond ring.

QUEEN. That might a mistress wear.

ROSA. Still brighter jewels have I in my children.
If these suffice not, lo! a marriage record,
That *proves* me what I am.

QUEEN. My children, Henry, Richard, Geoffrey!
Villain!
The sum of all the villanies of the world
Equals not this! I'll be revenged!
Water enough runs not in all the rivers
To quench what I will kindle!

[*Exit Queen in rage.*

ROSA. Alas! a woman's but a gilded moth,
With eyes and wings that tempt her to the flame.
This poor, insulted castaway is gone.
I shall be chid for telling her the secret,
That long hath slumbered, hid as in the grave;
And what if she were wife, and I the victim?
Why may not I be cheated, fooled, and damned
By the same glozing arts and whispering wiles?
She is more noble, beautiful, than I;
Some haughty princess, born to jewelled state,

And storied records of ancestral line,
Back reaching through the centuries ; cavaliers
Waited upon her, with high tossing plumes,
Pennons, and swords ; stout lances in the lists
Perchance were splintered ; gages were thrown down
And taken up to champion her beauty ;
And he who wore her colors in his cap
Sought death as lovers do their white-robed brides.
Could she be stolen like a foundling thus,
And hidden in some still retiracy,
Cajoled and bantered with, like Clifford's daughter,
And Christendom not rise in arms ? But I !
I knew him first, ere yet his eager lips
Had tasted pleasure's bowl ! My children, children !
Yet she hath children — sons — as well as I.
Perhaps we both in secret are mewed up
To minister — O God ! — to minister —
I shudder but to think upon my fate !
But no — his look — his voice — the priest — the altar —
His promises — his tenderness — no, *never !*

My heart, my faith go with him, and I'll trust him
Forever, yes, *forever!* [*Exit.*

SCENE II. — *Room in palace at Woodstock.* KING HENRY.

KING. William the Norman's lineage is cursed.
Sweet fruits and bitter grow upon one tree.
In youth, we follow hot and passionate joys;
In our fresh manhood, wars write bloody wrinkles
Upon our foreheads. We vex every sea
With keels, that, like to vultures, snuff their prey.
All lands whereon we set our conquering foot
Tremble and bleed. Nations shrink from the gaze
Of our fierce eyes, — shrink and give up the ghost.
Cities flame up against the midnight gloom,
And then go out in darkness. Crimes allure us;
Feuds kindle us. Sons against their sires
Flout angry banners, point rebellious swords,
Stir up revolts. Our wives and daughters mock us.
Our nobles shut their castle gates upon us,
And hurl defiance at us from their towers.
Our old age is a night of melancholy,

Wherein the learning cherished in our youth
Mixes itself like a pernicious drug
With every wayward action of our lives,
And smothers even our sleep with poisonous dreams.
Then do we penances and kneel at altars,
Build hermitages, temples, monasteries,
Gather the bones of martyrs and inurn them
In marble coffins, and then lie in state
Only to have our shrouds stripped from our corpses
By eldest sons, who leave our grooms and lacqueys
To bury us, without a priest to say
Masses for our sick souls. So let it be!
I am a Norman, and will trust my sword.
Prelates nor popes shall fright me from my throne,
Nor wrest my trident from me. I am England,
And England is the world!

Enter GLANVIL, *trembling and pale.*

KING. What spectre's this?

GLAN. I am
A leper! Look! like Naaman's blighted hand,
Both mine are white as snow!

KING. A leper?

GLAN. Banished from all society of my kind.
An interdict is put upon your kingdom,
The Clarendon constitutions abrogated,
All they who signed them from their oaths absolved,
And thunders spiritual above thy head
Hang, waiting thy repentance. O my king!
For one brief moment throw away your pride;
Bow to the storm. An excommunicate,
Too late to save himself, prays to the king
To have mercy on the king!
Bow low in the dust, and save thee from this curse!

KING. To him, my servant, my abjuring friend,
The vilest of all traitors? Never! Never!

Enter another messenger.

Nay, spare not! Croak thy damned announcement forth!
Thou bird of evil omen, utter it —
Scream it aloud! The echo shall be "Becket!"
Earth hath not in her caverns left a couch

Where lies an echo can say aught but " Becket ! "
So, shriek it, villain — give it air — " Becket ! "

MESS. My liege, the archbishop of Canterbury forbids
The bans betwixt Henry, thy eldest son,
And his affianced, Marguerite of France.
The princess, too sends word none but the primate
Shall set the crown upon her virgin forehead.

[*Exit messenger*

KING. Leave us, caitiff ! The butterfly ! the parrot !
When with our royal hands we bought the jewels
To decorate this Gallic popinjay,
And silks to flaunt her in, to send us word
She will — she will not ! Would it were her shroud,
And not her festive robe ! How oft I've heard it said
Ingratitude, upspringing like the nettle,
Chokes the best soil ; but that it grew in heaven,
And could put on the semblance of a flower
An angel might stretch forth his hand to pluck,
Till now, — I never could believe.

[*Scene closes.*

5

SCENE III. — *Council hall in the palace at Westminster. Curtain rises and discloses the council engaged in the trial of the primate. King, bishops, barons, sheriffs, and other officers.*

KING. Barons and prelates, ye have heard the charges
Preferred against the late lord chancellor.
He hath been cited to appear in court,
But wrapt in pride, contemning still the law,
Or shrinking from the exposure of his guilt,
He heedeth not our summons. If no friend
Or counsellor of his present himself
To answer for him, sentence must be passed.

WIN. My sovereign lord, I am the archbishop's friend,
By him commissioned to propose such terms
As may seem fit in this extremity.
The primate pleads his innocence, denies
All accusations that impeach his faith ;
Yet for the sake of peace, by my advice,
To break down every barrier 'twixt the king

And his obedience, he offers here
In full discharge to pay two thousand marks.

King. It well appears by evidence, the theft
Is four and forty thousand. Why should we
Compound this felony and forgive this wrong
For such a pittance as the twentieth part
Of that huge sum? Why doth he not appear
And answer for himself?
What say ye, lords and prelates, — is he guilty?

The barons all nod their assent; also the Archbishop of York *and the* Bishop of London; *the other prelates stand motionless.*

My lord of Winchester, how now? Are you
And your co-prelates here willing to stand
The sponsors of our ancient laws?

Win. [*Looking timidly at the other bishops.*]
My liege —

King. Nay, tell us — the time presses — will ye be
Supporters of the customs of this kingdom?
Ay, or no, speak!

WIN. My most dread lord, we will.

KING. All?

[*They all nod their approval.*

Enter ARCHBISHOP OF CANTERBURY *bearing aloft a large cross, followed by a train of priests and monks. He advances to the middle of the hall, glances coldly around upon the prelates, and then fixes his eyes upon the king, who starts back and turns pale, while the bishops cluster together and stand motionless.*

ARCH. Say, what means this?
Who says I dare not face this trembling king,
And these pale, quivering minions of his court?
Behold I come armed with this holy symbol,
Token of agony and bitter death,
Whose touch can scathe the throne and blast the sceptre,
Through all the kingdoms where the incarnate God
Is owned and feared of men. These hands are clean;
This heart is stainless of offence; this brow
Was never furrowed by the sharp remorse
That waiteth on a guilty solitude.
He who impleads me falsifies his word;

All witnesses appearing on their oath
To testify against me are base liars,
Whom God will punish with his direst vengeance.
Woe, woe, and lamentation on his head,
A hissing and a scoff shall be the wretch,
Shunned by all men, an outcast in all lands,
Who persecutes me here. Kings can destroy
The body ; but the blood of martyrs spilled
Shall rise in vapors till it stain the heavens,
And fall in rain till all the swelling rivers
Shall crimson every lip that drinks. Woe ! woe !
Sorrow and desolation !

KING. Peace, blusterer ! Am I perjured and a liar ?

ARCH. I know thy functions and thine attributes.
Once at thy bidding, I renounced my oath ;
'Twas the last time. I charge thee to thy face
With rank oppressions and with secret sins.
Where is the Clifford's daughter, once beguiled
With promises that melted from thy lips ;
And what were they but perjuries, my lord ?

KING. Alms thief, filcher of widows' mites, and robber
Of baronies and deaneries — bigot — knave —
What ho! arrest him!

[*The officers of the court approach, but hesitate.*

ARCH. Off, ye impious hands!
Off, palsy-stricken minions, imps of darkness!

KING. Hold, brawling priest! Proceed we now, my lords,
And you, my loyal bishops, with the vote.

ARCH. Tarry awhile! king, barons, laics all,
Vote what ye choose, pass sentence as ye will;
But you, suffragans, do I here inhibit.
This blow, thus aimed at me, must fall on you
And on the church. In Christ's name, I command you,
Sit not in judgment on me. Leave the court.

KING. Stay, on your fealty. If any go,
I'll send him to the Tower, and confiscate
His goods.

ARCH. Go, as you love your souls!

If any stay, I'll banish him to hell,
Where he shall wail, howl, curse, and gnash his teeth
Through torturing ages.

Advances towards them, waving the cross. The bishops move towards the door, when the king steps between them and the archbishop with his sword drawn.

KING. Shall the king stand, his hands behind his back,
For felons such as thou to pluck his beard?
Dost thou not know, in sacrilegious hands
The cross is lath, the crosier but a sheep-crook,
To make the rabble gape and franklins stare?
Flash not again on me those angry eyes;
I was not born to be outfaced by priests!
Out of my sight! Speak but another word,
And I will cleave that rebel head of thine!

To the bishops.

Stop, on the instant! On your lives, turn back!

ARCH. [*Moving toward the king.*] Henry Plantagenet,

I curse thee in the name of Rome!

At these words, the king lets fall his sword and stands trembling, while the bishops rush precipitately from the hall. Curtain falls.

ACT IV.

SCENE I.—*A room in archbishop's palace at Canterbury.* BECKET *reading a letter.*

ARCH. This letter, written by his holiness,
Commits the keys of Peter to my hands,
With power to bind and loose. Italy, France,
Navarre, Spain, Aquitaine, and Germany
Espouse my cause; England awaits my nod;
Nobles stand trembling, and the people gaze
With a wide wonder, as some baleful star
Blinded their eyes; Plantagenet alone,
Clad in the impenetrable mail of pride,
Struggles with fate.

Enter WINCHESTER. *He salutes* BECKET, *who regards him sternly.*

Judas betrayed his Lord.
Peter denied him, and then turned and wept.

Win. Like Peter, I am touched with keen remorse.
Forgive me, father!

Arch. Thou wast not bred to knightly exercises;
Fasting had made thee weak. Sceptres and crowns,
The pride of royalty, dazzled thine eyes.
A shirt of hair, the scourge, fasting, and prayer,
Are props of faith. Another time, my son,
Thou shalt do battle with a better heart.
You put a weapon in the devil's hands,
Deserting me, to wound yourself.

Win. Alas!
That I should quail before the wrath of Henry,
Forgetful of the wrath of God!

Arch. Thou art absolved. I pity thee and love thee.

Enter Archbishop of York.

I little thought, my noble lord of York,
So soon to see your grace under my roof.
Felons have little claim to courtesies
From those who judge them. But pray, pardon me!
Haply, I am arraigned on some new charge,
Your grace the high commissioner to hold

Court here at Canterbury?

YORK. My gracious lord,
Peaceful my mission is. I come a suitor,
A mediator 'twixt the church and state.
The king sends me —

ARCH. For forty thousand marks?
'Tis a small sum, — a very trifling sum;
And I am rich, but lavish, too,
Of dainty taste and frolicsome exploit.
I pray thee, lenp it me — but for a week.

YORK. Your grace is pleased to mock me,

ARCH. Or, belike,
The exchequer of his grace of York was drained
In preparation for the festival
Of the late coronation of prince Henry?

YORK. My mission is of peace. I have no heart,
Taunting or jesting, to provoke the edge
Of weapons which your grace can wield so well.
The king sends word that he remits the fine
Wrongfully levied; begs you to repair
To Woodstock (using all convenient haste),

Where he will make, in presence of his court,
Fit reparation. If 'tis your grace's wish,
He will consent the prince be crowned again.

ARCH. What! is the unction but a tennis-ball,
A school-boy's bauble, to be tossed about,
Vulgar with handling, as a May-day wreath?
Are men twice wedded to the self-same maid,
That rival priests may tie the mystic knot?
Are bishops twice invested, dying men
Twice shrived? My lord, my lord,
Be humble! for the purple heather towers
Never like the heaven-branching oak, but grows
Lowly and lovely, mantling the brown earth
With a wild grace and beauty of its own.
Look not too high, lest, stumbling, you should fall.

YORK. I thank your grace!

ARCH. And for the king's request,
If it shall suit my leisure, I will grant it.

YORK. I shall report your grace's answer. [*Exit.*

WIN. Strange!

ARCH. Fear! I've seen bloody battles in my time;

And when steeds neighed, and the brazen clarion
blared
Its wild notes in my ears, I felt a joy,
As I had been the echo of the blast
Startling the mountain silences; then rushed
Headlong upon the spear. Thus will I fight
God's battles!

Enter GLANVIL. *At sight of him,* BECKET *and* WINCHESTER *avert their faces and cross themselves.* GLANVIL, *advancing toward* BECKET, *kneels with his head bowed, his hands uplifted in supplication.*

GLAN. My gracious lord,
Hear me! I supplicate on bended knee
For absolution from this awful doom.
This curse — 'tis on my head — here at my heart,
Sunk like a stone. I do repent! Restore me!

ARCH. Crawling worm,
Reptile, slimy yet toothless, venomous without sting,
Hateful as abject! cockatrice! The Saxon,
The churl, the Syrian sets his heel upon thee,
And it shall bruise thy head. Out of my sight!

[*Exit* GLANVIL.

WIN. My lord!

ARCH. I know what thou wouldst say. My master
Was pitiful, tender, forgiving; I
Am proud, remorseless. Winchester,
He was a God; I am a sinful man,
Sprung from a race, whose high, rebellious blood
Burns 'mid the sands of Syria. O my God,
How often do I lay the crook aside
To bear the sword! Yet in the temple once,
When they who bought and sold defiled the place,
He drove them from its portals with a scourge,
And with a holy scorn o'erthrew their seats,
Spurning their money and their merchandise.
'Twas his example; I will follow it.

[*Exeunt.*

SCENE II.—*Palace at Woodstock. Enter* KING HENRY.

KING. Treason lurks in the castle, murder in the hold;
Disorder is the order of the realm;
Priests pry into my eyes with steel-cold glances,

Nobles desert me ; all the provinces
Are up in arms ; my sons thirst for my blood.
I am a captive led in Becket's train.

Enter GLANVIL, *dejectedly.*

And did he not absolve thee from the curse ?

GLAN. Think not of me. Make peace with him! Prop up
Your tottering throne!

KING. The throne is like the hills,
With roots that lie beneath the sunless caves
Of British seas.

GLAN. Alas! the roots are cursed.
No dews fall on them, no heaven-dropping rains;
Sapless and lifeless. Earth, their bed no longer,
Is now their grave.

KING. You talk in riddles, Glanvil.

GLAN. Know, then, this war with Becket and the church
Will overturn your throne, your bright crown jewels
Scatter o'er all the earth, to be up-gathered
By petty princes and invidious barons,

Who now, far off, with hate-envenomed eyes
Behold your state.

KING. I bear the sword of William.

GLAN. When plagues steal through your cities in the night,
Or death-angel — his hand upon the latch,
His foot upon the threshold of your dwelling —
Stands with masked features, will a soldier's brand
Pierce through the invisible mail of the invader,
And reach his heart?

Enter BECKET, *at sight of whom* GLANVIL *trembles violently and steals out of the apartment.* BECKET *advances haughtily, looking sternly at the king.*

ARCH. Much need hast thou, my son,
Of ghostly counsel. I can probe your wound,
Even to the quick. The caustic first, my son,
And then the oil and wine. Great was your sin.

KING. I will confess, my lord!

ARCH. Kneel!

KING. To thee?

ARCH. To God!

I am a worm, a sinful worm. The spear
Levelled at me pierced holy mother church.
The frauds, false accusations, perjuries —

KING. I will not hear it from thee!

Enter a messenger, who hands a letter to the king. He breaks the seal and reads it.

Ha!
I am free at last from this accursed thraldom!
This letter from the pope solicits aid —

ARCH. The pope! — to thee!

KING. From the pope Pascal third.
His holiness —

ARCH. The anti-pope! the wretch!
The usurper!

KING. I will throw into the scale
My trenchant sword. He shall keep Peter's keys.
I will keep him. On penalty of death,
I banish thee beyond the British seas!
Linger not! for the messengers of fate
Are on thy track! We lack a Saxon saint!

ARCH. My lord, I go. Victor, I will return!

Then shall you sue for mercy on your knees,
And hold my stirrup as I mount my palfrey,
In honor of the God you now blaspheme.
Then, if my name be added to the roll
Of blessed martyrs, you shall seek my shrine,
And monks at midnight on your naked shoulders
Shall lash you, as you kneel above my bones.

[*Exit* BECKET.

ACT V.

SCENE I. — ROSAMOND'S *tower.* ROSAMOND *weeping. Enter* KING HENRY. ROSAMOND *coldly extends her hand.*

KING. What means this chill, unwelcome courtesy?
And weeping? What can ail thee? Well-a-day!
The cottage was a blithesome place; this tower
Is cheerless, damp, and chill; the tapestry
Mildewed and old. Vines cannot climb so high;
And sunbeams, struggling through the deep embrasures,
Go out in darkness.

ROSA. I love darkness now.

It sorts with the complexion of my thoughts.

KING. Sweet wife —

ROSA. How many wives hast thou, my lord?
Two dwell at Woodstock. Say, how many more?
Doth every royal castle hide two wives?
Are Westminster and Winchester provided
Each with a double wife? One wife, one queen,
Each with a brace of princes at her girdle,
To furnish the succession of one throne?

KING. I will be plain with thee.

ROSA. The heaviest truth falls lightest.

KING. Dearest wife,
First loved — loved only — cherished as these eyes —

ROSA. No fond endearments, lord, nothing but truth,
Sharp as a lance — truth with death-dealing edge.

KING. Nothing but truth. Pray hear me, Rosamond.
My heart was all my own; this gave I thee.
My sceptre, crown, and royalty belonged
To England and the world —

ROSA. Go on — tell all!
KING. To Eleanora, I have given these last —
ROSA. What, the succession? Is she then the queen?
O broken heart! O evil-boding dreams!
Were ye more truthful than a great king's oath?
Alas! alas! my worst fears are too light
To carry such a load! No lingering hope
To let me gently down into the grave!
And I the victim of that jeering world
To scoff and point and hiss at all my life,
And trample on my grave and call me strumpet,
Till my dead ear awake, my shrouded limbs
Quiver with shame. O thou remorseless king!
Behold me here — a tempest-shattered flower,
Withering and sapless, severed from the stem,
Waiting the fury of the whirling blast!
Remember the lone garden, the hushed hour,
The tears that fell, the passion-throbbing kisses
That stifled even the praises of your lips,
As my poor ringlets tendriled round your fingers!

Remember all your pledges and your vows,
Repeated by the echoes of the night
That haunted there the swiftly-lapsing brook,
Whose waters had an undertone of love,
So like a dream I hear it in my sleep;
My doubts remember sweetly reassured —
My flight and fluttering fears — the saintly priest —
The altar, tapers, silent witnesses —
The firm responses and the deep amen
That sealed the hasty bond — alas! alas!
All broken like a thread of brittle wax!
Remember our last meeting! Spare — oh, spare
My sons! Cast me like a vile weed to drift
At the rude pleasure of the random wind,
But save them — save them, and I die content!

[*Weeps passionately.*

KING. (*With deep emotion.*) O Rosamond,
The wrong I did thee, bottomless as the sea,
All sorrow — all repentance swallows up.
I loved thee better than I loved my soul.
Still this one treasure hid I from the world,

Still clung to this too flattering, flattering dream,
That on some glorious coronation-morn
Thy lovely forehead, making jewels dim,
Thy brown hair, turning sunshine into shadow,
Should cluster 'round the shoulders of a queen.
But evil thoughts, distemperate love of power
Or fate to punish pride lured me astray,
To lose me in a desolate, lone wild.
Faltering, I sought to tell thee of this wrong,
But dared not. Troubles came, and family broils;
Distractions rent the vitals of my kingdom;
Thorns in my pillow, daggers at my heart.
Too selfishly I hoarded up our secret;
And now forgive — forgive me, Rosamond!
Queen canst thou never be; and these my sons,
My sole legitimate issue, follow never
In the true line of sovereignty. But stay,
My wife — my gentle Rosamond, — oh, stay —
Our home —

ROSA. This is the cruelest wrong of all!
Even wedlock is polluted, and our bed,

Defiled and loathsome, can be sacred now
But in the memories of my innocence,
And consecrations of a mother's joys.
Here from the world, a poor, crushed penitent,
To Godstow's convent I'll betake myself;
There will I dwell, a white and spotless nun.
High walls I'll place between my life and me;
My knees shall wear its rugged floors of stone
To marble smoothness, and my tears shall fret
In the gray granite channels of remorse.
Farewell!

[*Exit* ROSAMOND.

KING. Thus the last solace of a thorny life
Is plucked from me. I cannot turn my head
But spectres of injustice haunt my eyes.
Friends turn their backs upon me. Courtiers' smiles
Are marks for treachery. My queen plots treasons;
Henry and Richard, mad incendiaries,
Set castles ablaze, and, in the dead of night,
Run from the flames, leaving upon their track
A cry of women hurrying from their homes.

I cannot hold a chalice to my lips,
But poison bubbles down upon its brim.
O Rosamond, thou art too well avenged!

[*Exit*

SCENE II. — *The queen's apartments at Woodstock.* QUEEN ELEANOR.

QUEEN. I've kindled feuds betwixt the king and Henry.
Wars are abroad, distractions in the kingdom!
Divided counsels, desolated vineyards,
Castles dismantled, garrisons dislodged,
Churches in flames, and city walls thrown down!

Enter KING HENRY.

KING. What, in heroics, my fair queen? A miracle
Or a mystery? This is too small a stage
For royal buskins.

QUEEN. Acting now, my lord,
Has ceased to be a pastime to me. Action —
Definitive, bold action suits me best;
And on that stage I will have kings and queens;

The stake shall be for duchies and for kingdoms;
The end be desolation and wide woe.

KING. What may this mean? Thy cheek is flushed with rage,
And thy words hiss like serpents.

QUEEN. And my speech
Doth answer hiss for hiss.

KING. (*Bitterly.*) We strangle snakes.

QUEEN. That will I with this hand, though every scale
Were barbed like a lance. Nothing makes amends.
No taunts, no curses from a sulphurous tongue,
Dipped in the fires of hell and forked with poisons,
Can match this insult and this scathing wrong;
The bed of ocean cannot hold the hate,
Nor the void heavens can echo the despite
And loathing that I feel for thee.

KING. For me?
If thou do love thy life, beware! beware!
For, as I am innocent of any guile,
I will not brook a scourge upon my back

For any prim and idle gallantries
That knighthood hath contrived.

QUEEN. Then do thy worst.
Thou innocent! to call me wedded wife!
Thou, in the general eye of Christendom,
To crown me by thy side, and trumpet me
In every court the mistress of thy kingdom,
Call me the lawful mother of thy children,
Then drop me from the highest summit down
To deepest hells of shame; while in yon cottage
A fruitful spouse tarries impatiently,
Until her shapely princes shall be grown —
She, taught to cast her country garments off,
To sing, to dance, to courtesy to her dukes,
Give one cold hand to bishops and to earls,
And in the other hold a papal bull,
Absolving Henry from his vows to me,
Which shall be read on coronation day
By York to his suffragans!

KING. Peace, beldam!
Say, what if I should choose

To keep a songster in a bowery nook
To lull the hours your cursed passion ruffles —
If I should feed it from my hand and pet it
Till it grew tame and wonted to my touch,
Should Eleanora of Guienne say nay ?
She, who, when wife of Louis, king of France,
Did cast a shadow o'er the Dauphin's title,
Which every poet set to ribald rhyme,
From Auvergne to Navarre, from sea to sea ;
And for which crime, king Louis cast her off
To be the curse and penance of my life ?

QUEEN. O cruel, cold Plantagenet,
To help me sin, and, when repentance came,
Then throw my trespasses into my face
After long years devoted to thy bed ;
After I'd borne thee sons and soft-eyed daughters,
And nursed them tenderly, as lowly mothers
Fondle their issue, — standing by their bedside
In anguished hours of sickness, day and night,
Till God late pardoned what thou first forgave !
Cruel and brutal king ! O God, that I

The mistress of Poitou and Gascony,
The owner of the proudest, richest dower
That the sun looked on circling the fair globe —
That I, to save a quarrel, should submit
To be made landless, tenantless, a beggar,
By him who swore to guard me with his sword,
And then, because I graced this fog-dimmed isle
With arts and letters and such courtesies
As her beer-swilling boors not knew before,
Should be called actress, woman-troubadour!
'Tis pitiless and cruel as the grave!
Yet this I could have borne to save my children.
But that same baggage yonder, in the woods —
Ay, when I learned how she had thrust herself
And her young kites between us and a crown,
And made us the chief mockery of the world, —
How, by her marriage, other villanies
Were overtopped —

KING. Hold, woman, it is false!

QUEEN. It is not false!

KING. Who told thee it is true?

QUEEN. Her precious self!

KING. Never! never! never!

QUEEN. She did; showed me her pledges of it,
Her trumpery children, wedding ring, and trinkets;
Her keepsakes, crumpled parchment —

KING. Marriage record?

QUEEN. Ay, record! record! brave Plantagenet!
Now you are pale —

KING. Boy!

Enter page.

Summon the mareschal — quick!

[*Exit page.*

If two must call a third to keep a secret,
Look, it shall go no further! Here's an end.

Enter MARESCHAL.

Arrest her, and convey her instantly
Unto our royal seat of Winchester;
There keep her close.

MAR. What, sire! the queen? my lady?

KING. No words! Do as I bid thee.

[MARESCHAL *hesitates.*

Instantly!

[MARESCHAL *leads her off.*

Would that our Gallic cousin had her back!

Enter GLANVIL.

GLAN. Did you not send an embassy to the pope,
The choicest flower of your nobility
To offer charges against Becket there?

KING. We did; hast thou heard any news from them?

GLAN. His Holiness turned a cold shoulder on them
Till Becket's couriers had audience,
And then —

KING. Hell and confusion! Whence this news?

GLAN. From Clare, who, in a furious fit of rage,
Turned his back on the pope, left his compeers,
And forthwith sailed for England. Let him tell
In his own words what I shall ill translate;
Anon he will be here.

Enter EARL CLARE.

KING. Earl Clare, is't true
This demi-pope postponed your audience
Till Becket's shaveling factors could be heard?

CLARE. The matter's true; the manner of it worse.
The pope, seated in state, high and majestical,
Like great Canute when he chained up the sea,
Bowed apostolically cold, and said, —
"My lords, pray pardon me — some other time,
My lords. I have some high ambassadors,
Come from his grace of Canterbury here,
Who, as you know, may not be asked to wait.
Tell your good king, — Nay, come again to-morrow;
And if his grace's couriers have concluded,
Why, then," — here like cross-bow bolt I shot
Out of the presence, leaving my co-mates
To call to-morrow and next day and next,
Till Becket's —

KING. Clare, I'll be revenged for this!
Long scores I'll quit; I'll have another pope,
Or better we have none!

CLARE. At Soissons, Becket,
Under the care of Philip, earl of Flanders,
And the invidious Louis, king of France,
Lives in such stately, high magnificence,
That princes show like beggars to his state.

KING. My lord justiciary, I here decree
That all the revenues of Canterbury
Shall be sequestered.

GLAN. Tarry, my lord, awhile
Tarry, I do beseech you!

KING. Our decree
Is passed; the sanction of it be our sword.
And hark ye, lords! the hospitality
Of France, pope Alexander, and earl Philip,
Shall entertain the primate's poor relations
And his domestics, whom I banish all.
This order, Glanvil, see thou executed;
And cause each one to take a solemn oath
That straightway he'll resort to Pontigny,
And join his princely patron.

GLAN. O my lord,
I pray you hear me speak!

KING. I'll nothing hear!
Nothing but the assurance it is done!
Four hundred beggars thus feed at his cost,
Till frogs and locusts swallow up his pride.
It is our sovereign will that no appeal
Be taken to the primate or the pope.
If any man an interdict from either
Dare bring into this kingdom, he shall be
Held as a traitor. See thou it is done,
And executed to the direst stretch
And sanction of my power.

GLAN. I'll stretch it till,
Like a spent bow-string, it shall snap asunder.

KING. Mine be the loss; now, archer, on thy life,
Draw the shaft to the head!

[*Exit* GLANVIL. *King taken suddenly ill.*

KING. It ends where it began. The primate's king.
The royalties, the glories, the prescriptions,
The bended knee, the loyal-beating heart,

The swelling shout of the glad multitude
That's musical as the " all hail " of the spheres, —
These — these are Becket's, but no longer mine.

Enter ARCHBISHOP OF YORK, REGINALD FITZ URSE, WILLIAM DE TRACI, HUGH DE MOREVILLE, RICHARD BRITO, *and other knights and gentlemen.*

What, hath the primate's arrow pierced thee, too ?
The wounded only are so pale, my lord.

YORK. I am suspended from all exercise
Of spiritual functions.

KING. So am I, my lord,
Suspended from the functions of a king.

Enter BISHOPS OF SALISBURY *and* LONDON.

And lo ! two shadows of the prelacy !
Say, are ye, too, suspended ?

SAL. Worse than that,
My liege ; we're excommunicated.

KING. When will it end ?

YORK. Never — while Becket lives,
Never can England and the world know rest !

KING. Of all the servants feeding at my table,
Is there no loving knight or gentleman
Whose zeal will rid me of this thankless prelate?

While the king is speaking, the four knights FITZ URSE, DE TRACI, DE MOREVILLE, *and* BRITO, *whisper together and then withdraw separately.*

Is there no friend, no leal and loyal heart
Still lingering round the throne? Not one! not one!

DE TRACI. Let us retire into the wood together.

BRITO. 'Twere well we did. The king is very ill.

FITZ URSE. And must have medicines. Come!

Enter messenger, hurriedly.

MES. My liege!

KING. Despatch thine errand!

MES. 'Tis so dire
Words cannot utter it!

KING. Speak, on your life!

MES. The prince of Wales, my lord —

KING. What of the prince?

MES. He died at Martel Castle yesterday.

Your name was on his lips with his last breath;
Dying, he took this ring from off his finger,
And whispered, "Carry it unto my father,
And beg him keep it as a little token
Of Harry's penitence."

KING. I banished him;
I am his murderer! Alas! my son!
Atonement cannot reach it. Other crimes
Are angels pointing to the gates of heaven.
Repentance, though it travel with the light,
Can never overtake it.
Look at these walls! they sweat with drops of blood;
They fall upon my garments, stain my crown!
Written on all the stars, letters of blood
Do take the shape of that one horrible word,
Remorse — remorse — remorse!

He is led out by YORK *and* CLARE.

SCENE III. *A large oak in the park, near the palace-gate. Enter* FITZ URSE *and* DE TRACI *from opposite sides.*

FITZ. Where are the other two?

DE TRACI. I cannot tell.
This is the rock and this the spreading oak,
Our place of meeting; sit we down awhile.
What think you, have they failed us?

FITZ. No; look yonder!

Enter DE MOREVILLE *and* BRITO.

Ye are late.

BRITO. We missed the place.

FITZ. Dost think the king
Spoke from a passionate heat, or a fixed mind,
Deliberately intending all his words
Gave warrant of? What sayest thou, de Traci?

DE TRACI. His Grace of York first hinted at the deed,
With a sharp, eager look upon the king.
He meant—

BRITO. Blood!

DE MORE. His eyes said it!

DE TRACI. And the king—

FITZ. Echoed his meaning. Shall we kill this priest?

DE TRACI. If they relent, then we are murderers.

BRITO. If they be steadfast, we are dukes and earls;
I'll stake my dagger on the chance.

DE MORE. I mine.

FITZ. De Traci — thou ?

DE TRACI. A dukedom or a grave.

BRITO. 'Twere but a priest the less !

DE MORE. And priests are vermin.

FITZ. Enough ! he dies !

SCENE IV. *Room in the palace of* ARCHBISHOP OF CANTERBURY. *Enter* ARCHBISHOP.

ARCH. Again in England, and again restored !
A lay tribunal persecuted Christ;
He triumphed, and I triumphed by his grace.
Soon as I set my foot upon the island,
The inhabitants with green boughs welcomed me,
Hailed me with acclamations and hosannas;
And all the dusty way was thronged with priests
And laics honoring me. The populace

Shouted in city-streets, "Long live the primate,"
As I had been the king. The church is safe,
Her patrimony rendered back to me;
Her priesthoods, benefices, honors, lands,
Temples and palaces and jurisdictions.
All, all are safe. The king rules by the church;
The ministers, absolved, now execute
Their offices by order of the church.

Enter BISHOP OF WINCHESTER.

How fares the king, my lord of Winchester?

WIN. Since his late illness he's no more himself;
His eye is wild, his voice with passion trembles;
He mutters things disordered in his sleep,
And rates his ministers and barons all.
The day he helped your grace to mount your palfrey,
He most unmercifully beat his groom,
Drove Glanvil from his presence with drawn sword,
And railed and swore against ecclesiastics
So madly, that his chaplain fled the palace.
He calleth thee a traitor and a rebel —

ARCH. I humbled him but for the church's honor,

Not for the exaltation of a worm.
It was my office that he helped to mount,
Not my poor, sinful self. I pity him.
When, like an eagle with a broken wing,
His eye no longer blazing toward the sun,
Plantagenet fell fluttering to the ground,
I wept to look upon the spectacle.
But by regeneration shall the eagle
Be changed into a dove, the wolf to a lamb.
This knew I in my banishment and shame,
And this shall Henry know ; this York shall know,
Robert de Broc, and Nigel de Sackville,
And all who aided in that blasphemy
They called the coronation of the prince ;
Taking the royal unction from his head,
By which alone a king can reign in England,
The primate only can administer.
I have suspended York, the chief offender ;
The rest are excommunicated.

WIN. My lord ?

ARCH. Even by their names, as Henry's ministers

Were one by one driven from the anchorage
And blessed haven of the church.

WIN. Your grace
Would issue thus a fearful proclamation
Of open, horrible war.

ARCH. Dost thou forget
The number of God's chariots, Winchester,
His legioned cherubim? If there be war,
These win — faith wins — the primate wins.
God's enemies — my enemies — shall perish!
The horse and rider rolled beneath the sea.

Enter GRIM, *his cross-bearer.*

GRIM. My lord, I see without four knights in a
mor!
There's murder in their looks!

ARCH. Go, Winchester!
Tarry not! Fly!

[*Exit* WINCHESTER.

Why dost thou start so, Grim? Why dost thou
shiver,

As if some inward agony or fear
Thrilled thee?

GRIM. My lord, I fear these ruffians!

ARCH. I have no fear;
I wear the harness and the shield of Christ.
Roman nor Jew He fled from, nor will I.
They crucified Him; and the mocking thorns,
Transfigured like Himself, became a crown
Of everlasting glory. Martyrs have crowns
Second in brightness only to their Master's.
Hark! I hear singing.

GRIM. 'Tis the chant at vespers.
Take sanctuary in the church, my lord;
Shut thou the gates, and thou art safe.

ARCH. Dost bear
The cross of Jesus, and would'st thou take refuge
Within his temple, bar its doors, and make it
A citadel to garrison thee in?
Go thou! do penance! I'll to vespers, Grim;
But sanctuary only seek in prayer.

[*Exeunt.*

SCENE V. — *Evening. Interior of St. Benedict's church. The choir is heard chanting in the distance as* BECKET, *arrayed in his prelatical robes, kneels near the tomb of* ST. THEOBALD.

ARCH. (*Uplifting his hands.*)

Thou, from whose presence kings do shrink away,
In whose eye crowns are dim, — thou Blessed Son,
Whose brow once bled with thorns, but glitters now
With beams of glory ; and thou, holy Virgin,
Mother of God, ye, who have placed me here
Your British Zion to uphold and keep,
Oh, strengthen me ! And thou, the Holy Ghost,
Breathe on me, that my spirit may be clean.
Give me a flaming sword and angel-legions.
Ye saints and martyrs, quit your awful rest,
And throng to swell the numbers of the host
That fight the battles of the militant church.
Here I renew my vows ; and, if I turn
Or falter in your service, may I lie
Through the eternities beyond the reach
Of blessed intercession, hopeless, damned !

While he is praying, enter, hurriedly, the four conspirators in full armor and with swords drawn.

FITZ. Where is this rebel priest?

BECK. What means this cry,
Startling the echoes of this blessèd shrine?
And what unhallowed wretch, with clanging steel
And tossing plumes, dares desecrate these aisles,
Devoted to the holy rites of God —
The awful dwelling of the Prince of Peace?

FITZ. We dare!

BECK. Who are ye?

FITZ. Servants of the king!

BECK. Whom seek ye?

FITZ. The arch-rebel Becket!

BECK. By the dread sanction of the King of kings,
My Master, I command ye leave his temple!

FITZ. Not till we drag thee hence. Thou art a traitor!
Thy life is forfeit, and we come to take it!
So leave the altar ere this marble floor
Be crimsoned with its streams!

BECK. Back, murderous minions,

Ere from yonder heaven God's baleful lightnings
Flash in your faces!

FITZ. (*To the other conspirators.*) He will have it so!

They rush upon him with their swords. He disarms FITZ URSE, *takes his sword and defends himself with it.*

BRITO. (*Steps behind and stabs him in the side.*)
Thus dies a traitor!

BECKET *struggles and falls near the tomb of* ST. THEOBALD.

BECK. Thus dies a martyr, darkening with his blood
The monument of holy Theobald.
Bear witness thou, whose relics sleep beneath, —
Thou, who first taught my wandering feet the way,
My heart the truth, my darkened eyes the light,
That here I render cross and crosier up,
Stained only with these drops of martyrdom;
That I die fearless, fighting for the church,
My soul committing to the hands of God,
The blessed Mary, and her conquering Son!

[*He dies. Curtain falls.*

THE PHANTOM SHIP.

The olden days, when colonies were new,
Houses were huts, and churches arched with boughs
Of oaks that had been scathed by council-fires,
Saw nothing lovelier than Esther Vane, —
A farmer's daughter of Quinnipiac, —
Whose oval face and eye of hazel tint,
Hair of soft brown, with tendrils floating round
A brow of twilight and a cheek of dawn,
And such a shape as children in their dreams
See gliding down from heaven, — had such a charm,
That suitors came from many miles around,
Crossing her father's door-stone with such awe
As votaries feel in kneeling at a shrine.
From the deep fountain of a heart that loves
Not one but all, her nature bubbled up

And fell around her in a shower of joy.
They came and went, and still her bosom seemed
To sigh for others, never for itself.
Swift fled the summers; the wild strawberry,
Staining her fingers with its ruddy kiss,
Saw Esther and the lilies in one group
Stooping together, as the breath of June
Ruffled the meadow grass; and like the fruit,
And like the flower, the fragrance of her heart
Flew to the pines and cedars, where the birds
Caught it and warbled it among the boughs.
Happy the winters when her merry laugh
Startled the echoes of the sombre rock
That screened the settlement from the waste woods;
That winter happiest, bearing on its crest
Her sixteenth birthday like a white rose wreath,
When, dashing through the waters of the bay
One pleasant afternoon, a goodly ship,
Freighted with lives and merchandise, appeared.
Among the passengers, George Davenant,
A merchant's son from London, took his share

Of the rude welcome that the villagers
Gave to the ship and all who came in her.
Sun-blackened was his brow, glossy his beard,
Long, flowing in the wind like his wild locks;
And melancholy eyes, now blue, now dark,
As day and night had mingled in their depths;
Eyes, ambushed in long lashes, where there dwelt
Brain-pictures and the images of things
That poets conjure up to haunt the mind.
A man of musing, yet with conscious power,
Who waked upon occasion into act;
Proud, scholarly, and shy, with such a smile
As breaks in forests when a sunbeam glints
Upon their swarthy shadows suddenly,
Touching them with a gleam of tender light.
He brought a letter to John Davenport,
The minister, who only served one king —
The King of kings; who only knew one law —
God's law to man; who held the church and state
In his left hand, and scourged them with his right;
Yet gentle, too, and loving as a child

To such as needed help or sympathy
Or fellowship. He took the stranger home,
And, with a wilful fancy, clung to him,
Lodged him and petted him by turns, and prayed
Lovingly with him, tested him in Greek
With that fast-handed gripe of scholarship
Brought from the schools of Oxford at a time
When learning was the fibre of the heart;
Read him theologies from grimy books,
And, like a giant laying out his strength
To wrestle with a child, threw him amain
In dialectic wrath, then took him up,
Fondling his hurts, and poured in oil and wine.
Thus there sprung up, between the puritan
And passionate youth, a symmetry of love,
That sent a joy throughout the house, and breathed
A fragrance like the rose that nestled round
The study window in the month of June.
In that sweet month, so swift the days had flown,
As Davenant one evening to the beach
Had gone to meet the sea, his head bent low

Watching the traces of the ebbing tide,
He saw upon the eddies of the sand
A little foot-print, new and sharply cut,
And following, with a childish, quaint caprice,
The crescent sea-line close upon the foam.
He raised his head a little. Not far off,
Upon an ocean boulder that the waves
With immemorial touch had polished smooth,
There sat a girl, — he could not call her child,
So rounded was her figure with the grace
That years bring, blessing childhood into growth;
Scarce could he call her woman, when he saw
Her dimpled fingers showering pebbles out,
And heard her merry laughter as they fell
Bubbling like drops of rain into the sea.
Her only playmate here, the freshening breeze,
Tossed to and fro the brown locks of her hair,
That melted into auburn round her neck,
And, streaming backward, shimmered into gold.
Wondering, the youth stood looking at the maid.
She, whether by the shadow, startled up,

Or whether by some secret current hit
That flows between two forms with kindred souls,
Suddenly, like a bird that's taking wing,
Rose to her feet upon the slippery rock,
And glancing round, as if she sought escape,
A moment, and not finding any, smiled
And blushed, and leapt upon the dripping sand.

By explanations and apologies,
And kindly words from him to her, there grew
Betwixt them such acquaintance, that they traced
A homeward path together, parting not
Till he beneath the roof of Anthony Vane
Had safe bestowed the little treasure-trove
He found upon the shore.

From this hour, often, as the year rolled on,
Would George and Esther, wandering by the cove,
Snatch the pale shells from the pursuing surf,
Or watch the blackbirds hovering o'er the knolls,
Or upland plover hide her shining eggs
In the brown grass, or countless butterflies

Sparkling like gems ; and many a walk they took
Where the white thistle lured, — so few the flowers, —
Or the broom crowberry in soft, green mounds
Called to its springy couch to rest themselves,
Foot-weary with long rambles through the sand.
Swifter yet flew the days ; oh, happy days —
Days of a perfect summer, long yet short,
Under the shade of the woods in the fierce noon,
By reedy ripple of the river-bank,
In the long hour of twilight, when the moon
Hovering above the water, like a dream,
Waked it from sleep, or arrowy-light of stars
Fell on its silvery bosom in a shower ;
And later, when the wolf howled to the night,
They walked together on the moonlit shore.

It fell out at last
By slow degrees, his deeper culture wrought
A tinge of melancholy in her smile,
And shadows o'er her face would come and go —
The glimpses of his thoughts, exalting her

Into a loftier beauty, like to one
In merry mood who hears a sudden strain
Of mournful music floating on the wind,
Till its vibrations tingle through the frame,
And every nerve becomes a trembling chord
Keyed to the rapturous cadence. Even alone
She did not dwell upon familiar things
Of hearth, and home, and pleasures once so dear,
Only because she shared them with her friends,
But heard his voice, or saw him in her dreams,
Sleeping or waking.

Goodman Anthony Vane
Was puzzled at the change, and vexed at heart,
That Esther, who had been so merry once, —
Rather an echo, telling what she heard
Of pleasant voices, or a looking-glass
To multiply the shapes of household joys,
Than living creature in our world of care, —
Should seem another so unlike herself.
He could not speak to her as he was wont

Of homely things that hung about his life,
Or memories of the past that filled his soul,
She seemed so far off, and so spirit like,
As death had stepped between her and the world.

A word resolved his doubts. One Sabbath eve
As he sat looking into Esther's face,
Tracing the features of her mother there,
And wondering at the change, a gentle knock
Aroused him; and he rose to lift the latch,
While Esther, with instinctive woman's thought,
Fled at the summons. It was Davenant.
A little fluttered, with an undertone
Of calmness in his voice, he slid his hand,
So white and small, into the swarthy shade
Of Anthony's, that might have hid both his,
And looking at the farmer from still eyes,
And reading him as one might read a book,
Asked for his daughter. "I will call her, sir,"
Said Anthony; and sought to disengage
His hand and go, but Davenant held it fast,

And said, "No, no, it is not her I seek,
But you, her father." Then his heart broke forth
Into a wild confession of his love
That bore down Anthony with prevailing floods
Of eloquence that would not be withstood,
And ended in an ocean of sweet calm,
Where in a haven screened from angry waves,
Like two ships nestling side by side, they dropped
Safe anchors, well content.

The autumn came ;
The trees put on their holiday attire,
The barberry flashed from out her brambly hedge
Her scarlet berries in the robin's eye,
Tempting him from the alder, where he sat
A sentry for his fellows ; the wild pear
Grew yellow on the tallest branch, and fell,
Hiding among the fern and golden-rod ;
Nuts left their velvet couches in the burr,
And, to elude the squirrel, nestled down
In mosses, or beneath the rustling leaves.

The creeper on the elm grew crimson now;
Russet the oak; and the wild pigeon flew
Where the wide haze of Indian summer lay
Toward the far south-west; while here and there
Among the oracles of the fading year,
Esther their priestess and interpreter,
Although she knew it not, the scholar moved.

Meanwhile his cousin, Master Lamberton,
Builded a mighty ship, the like whereof
Had never dipped her keel in yonder bay.
Winter came on; and famine's haggard wings
Upon the blast spread with the blinding snows.
The people cried for bread; and Davenport
Stretched out his hands above their heads, and called
On God to give them bread. A ship or two,
In answer to his prayer, came beating in
From England, in December, laden with corn;
One brought a letter to George Davenant:
'Twas from his mother, bidding him come home,
In the first ship that left Quinnipiac,

To see his father die: 'twas but a word—
A timid wife's brief word of agony;
Prophetic, too, it seemed; the postscript told,
In the round hand of the executor,
The desolation of the house.

And now
They freighted the new ship with wampum-belt,
Furs, skins, and nuts, and fish; and Davenant,
Divided in his sorrow, weeping sore
At either loss—the future and the past,—
Flew to the house of Anthony Vane, and read
The letter both to Esther and to him.
A pallor, as of death, o'erspread her cheek.
"Parting from thee is very hard to bear,
And something warns me thou wilt not come back.
Fears haunt my dreams, and gloomy shadows flit
O'er pictures that I frame, at morn and eve,
To fill thine absence. 'Twas but yesterday
I saw a vessel on the open sea,
With living figure-head, whose lustrous eyes

Fixed their sad gaze on mine, and seemed to say,
'Too late — too late!' The winds piped in her
shrouds,
Till, wild with fear and questioning, I woke
To feel, as now, the burden of my life;
My planted cedar died, and the white bud
I named for thee is withered on the bush.
All things speak to me in an undertone
Of doubt and sadness." "Esther, I'll return
Right speedily, ere yon ambitious vine
We planted clamber to thy window-frame;
Thou'lt tend it for me, Esther, water it,
But not with tears, and give it thine own smiles
For sunshine; and remember God is good,
And loves the faithful heart that trusts in Him.
His days are swift; so, love, you'll wait for me."
"Go, George, I'll wait for you, though furious storms
Should drive you in mad circles round the world,
Dash you on coral-reefs, or buffet you
With breakers on the sands of tropic shores, —
Though years should toss between us, I will wait."

"Go, George," said Anthony, while his brawny arms
Embraced them both, and his lips worked with pain
As his eye fell on Esther, where she stood —
A glory lighting up a gloom. "Alas!
Alas!" said Davenant, "must I go, sweet heart,
As I have stayed, unwedded? Put a ring,
A mystic ring, upon thy finger, love,
And bid me go to-morrow." "Speak to him,"
Said Anthony, "the godly minister;
As he shall say, I pledge thee she shall do."

The day came for the sailing of the ship;
'Twas January, very stark and cold;
A fall of snow had hid the travelled ways;
Sleet hung the elms with glistering icicles;
Dun houses had put off their stainéd garb
For one of purest white. The little wharf,
Belted with shallops and with pinnaces,
Lay in the steel-cold air. While far away,
Towered in the background those two mighty rocks —
Ice-capped, snow-crowned, against the distant clouds,

And sending salutations to the sea.
Near the bleak shore lay the expectant ship;
Stout hearts had cut her way, for three long miles,
With saws and axes, through the solid ice,
And cleared the snow-drifts for her helpless keel
Far out where the bright waters of the sound
Welcomed her home. A drum-beat told the hour;
Men, women, children, gathered to the beach
To witness her departure. Every heart
Beat with its separate agony, or throbbed
With its own expectation from the shore.
Freed from her icy fetters, the good ship,
With her bow pointed seaward, had swung round,
When Davenport, surrounded by his flock,
Came forward and knelt down upon the ice,—
All kneeling round him,—and with upraised hands,
Called on the God of storms to throw his arms
Around the frail bark and her precious crew;
And, as his voice rose on the wintry air,
Swelling in hope, then sinking into doubt,
The multitude bowed down their heads and wept.

Then, stretching out his hands toward the shrouds
And fluttering sails, he blessed the ship, and said, —
"Almighty God! and if it be thy will
To bury these our loved ones in the sea,
Lo! they are thine; but save them."
Then Davenant led the maiden of his choice
From out that holy hush of worshippers,
Undaunted by the throng. She looked alone,
With earnest gaze fixed on her father's face,
Who came, his white hair streaming in the wind,
And pressed her outstretched hand with firm consent,
Kneeling beside the lovers as they joined
In holy wedlock their divided lives.

The ship moved out toward the open sea;
Sail after sail was spread before the wind;
Right gallantly she passed the wooded point,
The cross of St. George fluttering at her peak;
And slowly wended home the village folk,
Wondering and prophesying her return.

The winter passed; spring came with bud and bird,
And deepened into summer. Other ships
Came from the mother-land, and brought no news
Of her who sailed, freighted with good men's lives.
Friends in each other's faces looked and sighed;
Whispers grew audible in the market-place;
Doubt ripened into fear, fear into gloom.
From household altars many prayers went up,
That God would give them tidings of their friends.
No tidings came. "The ship is lost," they said;
"The ship is lost."

Meanwhile, in Anthony's house,
A settled stillness, like a twilight, reigned.
Calm, pale, and sometimes with a holy smile,—
As she, communing with her God, had learned
What others knew not — Esther moved about
Evermore musing; and by day or night,
When her vague spirit of unrest took wing,
It flew toward the sea. Nor did she go
Alone; but, like all other tender things

That think themselves unseen, and, happiest so,
Love solitude and liberty, yet roam
Under a hidden keeper, ever nigh,—
Never alone she went, but always lost.

A second June came, and one Sabbath day
The bell tolled for the funeral of the crew;
And Davenport to all the mourners preached,
Ranged in a circle round him, draped in black,
A funeral sermon like an ocean dirge;
But Esther sat in Anthony's pew, and wore
No outward demonstration of a grief,
Nor sobbed, nor shed a tear, nor bowed her head,
Till the amen that closed the service fell
Upon her ear like something she had heard
In childhood, or remembered in a dream.
The mourners left the house; the minister
Came down the pulpit stairs in gown and band,
And, moving toward her ere she was aware,
In benediction or in sympathy,
Laid his white hand upon her head and spake:

"Hope is an amaranth, Esther, when it blooms
In yon celestial regions, where no storms
Roll the capped breakers over sandy reefs,
Nor founder the frail bark in sight of land.
But interlace no myrtle, O my child;
No earthly vine should touch the shining flower
That makes the garland of the sons of light.
He is in Heaven, where, like the Prototype,
He waits the coming of his faithful bride.
Go home and weep. Christ wept, and so mayst thou."
He kissed her forehead, — it was cold as ice.
He touched her hand, — it was as white as snow.
Weeping, he saw that Esther could not weep.
Passive, she took the arm he proffered her,
And answered nothing to the words he spoke,
Nor knew the paths he led her by, nor felt
His presence till his absence called it back
As the house-door closed on him, and she heard
Her father sobbing; then her woman's heart
In sympathetic tenderness gushed forth,
And, sitting on his knee, she hid her face

With both her hands, and then the tears fell fast,
Like raindrops from a vine stirred by the wind.

That afternoon she wandered to the beach
And from the ocean boulder watched the sea.
A mournful smile flitted across her face,
As her eye caught the sea-birds in the clouds,
Or swooping on the wave-crest with mad wings,
Or wailing inland in long, shadowy trains.
The sun went down, but not a star shone out;
The cheerless heavens shrouded all the land,
Till sea and shore and sky were lost in one.
Yet she, whose life was sunless, loved the gloom;
Unknown the mysteries of sound and sense
Commingling essences impalpable;
Nor why the world-worn soul may gather strength
Through nature's ministering; nor why the sweep
Of the wild sea, the whirl of wind-swept leaves,
Or dash of torrents have the power to bring
This tribute of soul-healing. She felt not
The evening's chill; but, taking heart, she moved

With step more firm along the yielding sand.
The cross was heavy, bitter was the cup, —
Too bitter ; and, in agony of faith,
She questioned of the future, and she prayed
The desolation of her life might end.

Then the weird music of the waves did shape
Itself into a wild, impassioned voice,
And brought from out their depths unto her ear
A name she could not utter. 'Twas his name.
The faith of childhood lit her homeward way.
" It is God's promise he will yet return.
My husband, as I pledged thee, I will wait."
With these words on her lips, she reached her home ;
And with this burden, smiling, fell asleep.

It was June,
A pleasant afternoon, as on the sands
Esther pursued her customary walk,
When, suddenly, the sky was overcast ;
The air was sultry, and the bay was calm ;

But, now and then, hot gusts of stifling wind
Swept over it with ridges of black wave;
Aloft the winds blew fiercer than below;
Masses of pitchy vapor, mounting up
From the horizon, rolled across the heavens
Like a long funeral train. The gusts became
More frequent, charged with blinding clouds of dust,
Swooping upon the waters of the bay,
And breaking its black ridges into lines
Of foaming white. Flashes of lightning streaked
The gathering clouds with evanescent fires;
Thunders, that in low mutterings until now
Had spent their sullen wrath, crashed overhead;
The great drops hissed as they came whirling down,
Making deep channels in the moving sands;
While robes of mist hid rock and plain and sea.
'Twas a brief fury. Leaden vapors moved
Across the heavens; and azure specks were seen
In the dim west, and widening as the clouds
Dissolved in mist, the golden sunbeams smiled.

Amid the shattered fragments of the storm,

With downcast eyes, Esther turned slowly home.
Scarce had she left the beach, when her quick ear
Caught up a cry, like to an echo, faint
At first and far. It seemed a cry of fire,
Thrilling the village streets, and running wild
From house to house. See looked; and lo, they
came —
Men, women, children, sweeping toward the shore;
And, in the strange confusion of the din,
She gathered these two words, — "The ship! the
ship!"
Her heart leaped with a mighty throb of pain;
She pressed her hand against her side and sank
Down on the fragment of a rock hard by.
A mariner swept past — "The ship! the ship!"
"What ship?" she gasped. "Why, Master Lamber-
ton's,
That sailed so long ago. Dost thou not see
Her yonder, down the bay?" And he held out
His sun-burned hand and pointed toward the sound.
She looked, and uttered a sharp, piercing cry.

Her face was livid, as if struck with death ;
Or else some apparition, from the world
That God shuts out from this our world of sense,
Had fixed her eye and frozen it to stone.

A ship, — 'twas Lamberton's — in open sight,
Was beating into port against the wind
That blew almost a hurricane from the north ;
Sails set and ensign flying, on she came,
As if the wind was with her. Sailors stood —
Old weather-beaten men — and looked askance,
And, wondering, asked each other what it meant ;
While those unskilled in sea-craft breathed short prayers
Of thankfulness to God for bringing back
Their friends, whom they thought buried in the sea.
The children ran along the beach and cried, —
"There's a brave ship!" as, in the eye of the wind,
Under a cloud of canvas, she swept on ;
And a strange awe crept o'er the multitude,
As silently she moved through the crisp waves.

When she came nearer, they could see the crew
All standing at their posts upon the deck ;
And many knew the forms of those they loved.
Upon the ship's side stood a well-known shape,
In the same dress he wore when the ship sailed,
With that same earnest scholar's face, and waved
One hand to Esther, with the other hand
Over the ship's rail pointing to the deep.
She knew her husband, called him by his name.
No answer made he save the dear, sad smile
And mystic finger pointed to the sea.

The vessel came up to the harbor bar,
When a great cloud, around whose edges played
A light unearthly, settled slowly down
Upon her straining top-masts, and the wind
Piped out a dying requiem through her shrouds ;
And as the people looked in shuddering fear,
The top-sails melted, one by one, in air,
The great masts toppled, and the spars fell down
Noiselessly as a dream ; and last, the hull,

That sat so gracefully upon the waves,
Grew larger, dimmer, ghostlier, as it swelled —
Veiled in a mist that rose from out the sea,
And, faint and shadowy, wreathed its sombre folds
About the ship, hiding from mortal sight
Vessel and crew.

Then, like the Phantom Ship,
The people vanished from the spot. Alone,
No longer looking as with human eyes,
Esther went home. She did not seem to pine;
No longer did she wander by the sea,
But, like a mourning dove that has a haunt,
And loves it for its precious, bygone days,
And has a song that echoes to old nooks,
A few sweet, mellow notes of heart and home,
And has a love-eye full of tenderness, —
She nestled in her father's house, and blessed
His broken years, and smoothed his long decline.
The hope that fed her life melted away
With the dim shadow of the spectral ship.

Heaven's promise was fulfilled, and she would go
To him; he never could come back to her.
And Anthony Vane, who saw his daughter's hand
In everything that touched him, saw and felt
Her tender ministries, so dear to him
Were all that kept her yearning spirit back
From home and rest; and when he died, she passed
As gentle twilight fades to deepest night.

KING HACO'S FUNERAL.

King Haco on the bloody plain
  Fought all the weary day;
And when the sun sank in the main,
  His thegns around him lay
In scores; his life-blood flowed apace,
  Dim was his haggard eye,
And the cold dew-drops on his face
  Told that his end was nigh.
Fierce as the wolf's howl in the dark
  He heard the victor's song;
It fanned anew the lingering spark
  That now had slept so long.

Down to the water's edge he crept,
  Where, tossing on the bay,—

While at the helm the pilot slept, —
  His war-ship anchored lay.
He called aloud, " Ho! come ashore,
  And fetch from yonder field
The dead men lying in their gore;
  Fetch every helm and shield!"
They brought them dripping in their blood,
  The warriors cold and stark;
They brought the shields and helmets good
  Down to the dancing bark.

" Pile men and arms upon the deck,
  A sacrifice to Thor;
No bird shall feast upon the wreck
  Of Vikings slain in war!"
Ghastly the dead beneath the moon
  Stare from their hollow eyes;
The sea-blast pipes its wildest rune,
  The spray around him flies;
The sailors step ashore; the king
  Mounts to the deck in haste;

He was the only living thing
  To tempt the watery waste.

He ships the tiller, spreads the sail,
  And, as he quits the land,
He kindles in the freshening gale
  A fire with eager hand.
The dead men's weapons feed the flames
  That lick up streams of blood,
And from their shields the warrior's names
  Flash out upon the flood.
And forth between the rocky isles
  The ship flies, burning clear;
Among the dead he lies, and smiles
  To know his fate is near.

Aloud he sings a merry stave,
  And quaffs the ruddy wine,
While fiercer winds around him rave
  And whirl the sparkling brine.
"Ho! ho! high in Valhalla's Hall
  The gods drink to the brave!

'Tis thus that Thor and Odin call
  The Viking to his grave.
Ho! ho! the fire burns pure and free;
  It kindles sail and shroud!"
Thus in the middle of the sea
  Went down the Viking proud.

HAWTHORNE'S SLEEP.

LIKE a pure child the poet fell
  Into the arms of sleep ;
He heard around him sink and swell
  The music of the deep, —
The cadence of a far-off hymn
Haunting a forest dim.

An angel, borne on wings of light,
  As through the azure cope,
Athwart the watches of the night,
  He shot with downward slope,
Glancing the curtained casement through,
Kissed the majestic brow.

The morning at the window-pane
  Peeped in with merry eye,

Just looked and shuddered and amain
  Fled to the purple sky ;
For shadows, such as night knows not,
Were hovering round the spot.

ELDER BREWSTER'S PRAYER.

"Set down the bier, the head toward the west,"
  Whispered a white-haired man, as on they bore
  Along the hill that crowns the sea-worn shore
Another stricken brother to his rest;
"Set down the bier, and, with a holy trust,
Commit the loved one to his kindred dust."

Bleak raves the wind and hoarser breaks the surge;
  And through the bars of yonder rifted cloud
  The sunbeam flickers pale as in a shroud;
And nature has one voice, — a winter dirge.
Gently they lowered the coffin; then laid bare
Their heads to listen to the good man's prayer.

"O God," he said, "who keep'st the sunless deep,
  And mak'st it slumber like a new-born child,

Or dashest it along these rocks so wild, —
O God, forgive thy children that they weep;
Pardon the wavering faith, the broken vow;
Let thy hand stay the desolation now.

"Famine is in our bones, and snow and cold
Breathe on us; pestilence lets fly
Its arrows, and the smitten bleed and die.
One half our band here sleep beneath the mould.
Save but this remnant in its sore distress
To lift thy banner in the wilderness.

"Our wives, our children, and our gray-haired ones,
Oh, save them! bid the sick man from his couch
Arise and bless thee for the healing touch;
And from our number yet hew corner-stones
To grace thy temple in this shadowy land;
Let the hills praise thee, and this rocky strand."

Thus prayed he; and his voice died on the blast.
They filled the grave with earth moistened with tears,

To wait the dawn that follows all the years.
The patriarch sighed; and then his dim eye cast
Upon the long line of those new-made graves
Sprinkled with salt spray by the dashing waves.

He shook his palsied head, and pointing, spoke:
"Throw down the sods from every sloping mound,
And level with the surface of the ground
These witnesses of death's relentless stroke,
Lest to the red men of the woods they tell
How few there live, in counting those who fell."

With pious hands they bowed them to the spade;
The father o'er the ashes of his child,
The husband bending o'er his partner mild,
The youth above the cold brow of the maid;
And when their work was done, nor friend nor foe
Could point the spot where any slept below.

ANDERSONVILLE.

No blanket round his wasted limbs ;
  Under the rainy sky he slept ;
While, pointing his envenomed shafts,
  Around him Death, the archer, crept.
He dreamed of hunger, and held out
  His hand to clutch a little bread
That a white angel with a torch
  Among the living and the dead
Seemed bearing, smiling as he went.
  The vision waked him ; and he spied
The post-boy followed by a crowd
  Of famished prisoners, who cried
For letters, — letters from their friends.
  Crawling upon his hands and knees,

He hears his own name called ; and lo,
  A letter from his wife he sees !

Gasping for breath, he shrieked aloud,
  And, lost in nature's blind eclipse,
Faltering amid the suppliant crowd,
  Caught it and pressed it to his lips.
A guard who followed, red and wroth,
  And flourishing a rusty brand,
Reviled him with a taunting oath,
  And snatched the letter from his hand.
" First pay the postage, whining wretch ! "
  Despair had made the prisoner brave.
" Then give me back my money, sir !
  I am a captive, — not a slave.
You took my money and my clothes ;
  Take my life, too ; but let me know
How Mary and the children are,
  And I will bless you ere I go."

The very moonlight through his hands,
  As he stood supplicating, shone ;

And his sharp features shaped themselves
  Into a prayer ; and such a tone
Of anguish was there in his cry
  For wife and children, that the guard,
Thinking upon his own, passed by
  And left him swooning on the sward.
Beyond the " dead line " fell his head ;
  The eager sentry knew his mark ;
And, with a crash, the bullet sped
  Into his brain, — and all was dark.
Yet, when they turned his livid cheek
  Up toward the light, the pale lips smiled,
Kissing a picture, fair and meek,
  That held in either hand a child.

BLOOD.

You talk of blood and trace yourself
  Back to a Norman stock;
Shake in my face your dirty pelf
  And prate of Plymouth Rock.

You sneer at me with dainty lip
  Who are so slight and trim.
I drink the dregs of life; you sip
  The foam upon the brim.

Take care! for fortune has a wheel
  Which evermore revolves;
And hearts like mine are bows of steel
  Bent up to high resolves.

Take care! remember words are things,
  And all things have a germ;
A butterfly without its wings
  Is nothing but a worm.

ANTONINA.

Stay, let me look upon that brow,
Brown as the twilight flitting o'er a lake;
So lone and shadowy art thou
All fancies ripple in thy wake.

Thou glidest from me like a dream,
Thou gleamest on me like a pallid star;
O Antonina! faintest beam
Of starlight wandereth not so far.

Or in its flight 'twould grow so wan,
How could it warm my dull and shivering frame?
Smile, Antonina, as yon sun
Touches the westering cloud with flame.

LIFT UP THE BANNER.

Lift up the banner! fling its folds
  Wide on the breeze of east or west;
On every battle-field that holds
  A soldier's heart within its breast;
On hill-tops where the winds are strong
  To toss the glorious stars on high,
And add sphere-music to the song
  The poet heard in yonder sky.

Lift up the banner in the South!
  On Richmond's walls and Charleston's spires,
Above the grisly cannon's mouth,
  No longer blazing with the fires
Of livid hate and hellish spite;
  But, standing on the river-brink

Or ocean-rampart, guard the right
  While crumbling empires round us sink.

Lift up the banner in the North!
  Where the lakes battle with the blast,
Whence yon wild cataract, issuing forth,
  Wakes the provincial ear at last
With thunders that the gulf proclaims,
  Still echoing to the frozen sea,
That kindred blood feels kindred shames
  And Saxon hearts love liberty.

Lift up the banner! let it float
  Between the isles, around the capes;
O'er monitor and mailéd boat
  Of weird inventions, wizard shapes;
On rough seas and on calm; where'er
  A wheel can ply, a keel can ride:
No cheek beneath it pales with fear,
  All hearts beneath it beat with pride.

BRIDE BROOK.

A HERMIT in a solitude
  That heard few voices save its own,
A small brook, winding through a wood,
  Like a lost child, moaned sadly on ;
Few dimples on its face were seen,
  Save where the sunbeams, glancing through
The shadows of the evergreen,
  Kissed the light bubbles as they flew.

It had no name, this dainty brook,
  But Winthrop, in the merry reign
Of Charles, explored its deepest nook
  When cares of state perplexed his brain ;
Oft sauntering there with downcast eye,
  It soothed him, and he loved the spot ;

For nature had no mood so shy
  That gentle Winthrop shared it not.

One day a youth and maid he spied,
  Lovers employed in secret talk,
As up the brook, on either side
  In separate paths, they held their walk,
Now thoughtful, now in mimic strife;
  Forth stepped the magistrate, and smiled:
"Join hands! I make you man and wife!"
  Thus were they wedded in the wild.

Across the brook he kissed his bride,
  (And graver lips there claimed a fee;)
He never wandered from her side;
  A happy, loving wife was she.
And thus Bride Brook the stream was named
  And ever since that jocund day
Its voice is merry; and 'tis famed
  In prose and verse for miles away.

MY HOUSE.

By H. S. D.

I BUILDED up with patient care
  My house of pebbly whiteness,
And not a chink nor spot was there
  To whisper of its lightness;
With skill and taste, I chose in haste
  Rare gems the arts adorning;
Vines inlaced my windows graced
  With tinted rays of morning.

Bright waters sparkled in the sun
  From founts of graceful measure,
And rare exotics breathed thereon
  Incense of spicy treasure;

The ambush made by sylvan shade,
  Did woo each airy rover
To rest among with chirp and song,
  Brimming my song-cup over.

The humming bird, the butterfly,
  Ran riot o'er the flowers;
While insects, flitting in the rays
  Of sunshine, mocked the hours.
Ah! here, I cried, will I abide
  As free as bird above me,
Will chant my lay the livelong day,
  Nor ask a heart to love me.

The poet's shell alone shall tell
  Of fancied woe, and borrow
Its shadows from the early dawn
  That ushers in the morrow;
Thus will I live; to dreaming give
  The wealth of hope to mortals,
And paint the bliss of Paradise
  That opes the grave's sad portals.

MAJOR-GENERAL JOHN SEDGWICK.

IN MEMORIAM.

A LITTLE valley fenced by natural walls;
  Through it a brook winds toward the neighboring river;
A little grave-yard where the sunlight falls
  On green mounds, over which no willows shiver,
Nor leaves of pine that on the mountain's head
Keep the wild snow-drifts from their peaceful bed.

A spot beloved by all the country folk;
  Here Sedgwick lived, and here by many a token
Of look and word and smile and homely joke,
  They kept his image in their hearts unbroken,
Though few his visits now to that old home
Whose doors ajar invited all to come.

Chief of the Sixth Corps! in that silent house
  One gentle spirit, haunting it, there lingers;
Her clear eye kindles and her thoughts arouse
  At midnight, dreaming of thee; and her fingers
Grasp the brief telegrams that thrill the world,
Whene'er the Sixth Corps' banner is unfurled.

The clouds wept on that morning, when we met
  At the dear mansion house in Cornwall Hollow;
We said but little, yet our cheeks were wet
  With the proud tears that evermore will follow
The hearse that carries home the noble dead;
And here we laid thee in thy lowly bed.

Let the dust sleep among its kindred dust!
  Father and mother, loving friend and neighbor!
And let the mountain-pine, true to its trust,
  Even like the hero, buffet and belabor
The wintry blast upon the distant hill.
Forever hallowed be that spot and still!

Yet Sedgwick sleeps not there ; for soul like his
  Sleeps never after death. At once it enters
Into the living forms of all that is,
  Haunting the ages, lighting up the centres
Of crumbling states, and waning, wasting creeds,
And touching dead shapes into living deeds.

We bid thee not farewell ; cold as we are,
  We welcome thee in all familiar places ;
We see thee in the eagle, in the star,
  And hail thee in a thousand happy faces
That smile upon our flag, on land or sea
The symbol yet of faith and type of thee.

SEDGWICK'S SWORD.

We walked about the silent hall
  Treading the floor that Sedgwick trod;
We saw his picture on the wall,
  The saddle-cloth on which he rode;

The reins he held, the bridle-bit
  That checked his war-steed's furious way,
The sword — keen-tempered as his wit —
  Untarnished like that summer's day.

A golden-hilted, flashing blade,
  Stamped with his battles, old and new, —
A cunning work of art, that made
  A very noonday where it flew.

Soldiers who loved him gave the brand;
He bore it as a soldier should,
With an unfaltering, faithful hand,
And never stained with needless blood.

Forever let that hallowed steel,
Without a rust-mould or a flaw,
O'er us its fiery circles wheel,
The symbol of a living law.

Still may it pierce rebellion's breast,
The heart of innocence still guard,
And glow like sunset on the rest
So deep beneath yon grass-green sward.

WATER LILY.

By J. D. C.

Mantled in her silver vest,
Bride-like, lieth she at rest,
Pillowed on the water's breast;

Looking up with timid eye
At the cloud-ships sailing by
Through the sapphire-vaulted sky;

Joying in the elfin song
Of the winds, whose wailing throng
Sweep the placid lake along.

Thus, enthroned with regal sway,
Queen of golden-wingèd day,
Dreameth she her life away.

TRAILING ARBUTUS.

Sly loiterer 'mid the wintergreen,
  Hiding beneath capricious snows,
That by the hedge-row's russet screen
  Melt in the south wind as it blows;
Thy mantle is a rustling leaf,
  Gray mosses make thy frugal bed,
And sere grass hides thee, little thief,
  Under its scanty coverlid.

When didst thou blossom, pretty one?
  Beneath December's emerald ice
Thy buds were small, thy leaves were dun,
  The sunlight looked not in thine eyes.
Oh, tell me at what idle hour
  When other flowers are folded up,

Under what planetary power,
  Thy petal fills its scented cup!

Alack! what heart hadst thou to smile
  When the great hemlocks shiver so,
And oaks and maples frown the while,
  And scowling beeches, to and fro,
Whip their long arms to keep them lithe
  And bring the thin blood to their brows?
I marvel thou canst be so blithe
  With April to renew thy vows.

For April breaks them every year,
  Frowning upon thee, puny thing,
And scarcely stoops to kiss a tear,
  If to thine eye a tear should spring;
He trifles with thy rosy lips,
  With icy breath he chills thy breast,
And freezes to the very tips
  The leaves that nestle thee to rest.

Why should I blame thee? I have seen
  So many maidens do the same,
Loitering amid the wintergreen
  To hear some April breathe their name:
So have I seen their pink grow pale,
  And pale go fading into white;
So shivered as I heard the gale
  And felt the shades of coming night.

TO JOHN BRIGHT.

WHEN the crown pales and yonder throne
    Topples and sinks beneath the sea,
    When dukes are things of history,
And earls in memory live alone
Honored because a Villiers spoke,
    A Howard pleaded for a cause
    That sets the Law above the laws,
The people shall survive the yoke.

Go on, brave heart! the structure stands
    A monument through coming time;
    To thee the men of every clime
Uplift their voices and their hands;
Labor and honor now stand up
    By the same hearth-stone's ruddy glow,
    Drinking enchantments as they flow
Forever from truth's golden cup.

CLEMATIS.

In all the tangles of the woods
    Thy tender leaves and snowy flower,
    At morning or at evening hour,
Can touch the happiest, saddest moods.
How the brook loves thee! by its brink
    Vaulting above the glossy beech,
    Or stooping from its crest to reach
The brown wave, where the alders drink.

I liken thee to many things
    That please the eye and thrill the nerve:
    A woman in thy shy reserve,
A bird with bright and soaring wings,
A hope, a wish, a sentiment,
    An upward climbing heavenly dream,

When stars on dew-drops softly gleam,
And clouds are pictures of content.

Like a fond lover, in whose eye
All dresses suit the form and face
His fancy clothes with such a grace,
He never asks a reason why;
Like him I bless thee in the days
When first thy tendrils seek to climb,
In the white buds of summer time,
Or autumn's dim and shadowy haze.

Come, be my bower, and through thy leaves
Let all flower-kissing breezes blow;
And echoes from the brook below
Mix with the rustling of the sheaves.
Enter not here disturbing cares,
But lovers cheer thee with a smile,
Or, if a tear do drop the while,
It shall be thine as well as theirs.

TENNYSON.

PROPHET and poet of the day,
  Seer and maker of the time
  That lives foreshadowed in the rhyme
Whose echoes cannot die away ;

Lives in such pictures as the sun
  Paints on the welkin's purple rim
  In colors that shall not grow dim
When this our little day is done :

Long may the murmurs of the pine,
  Long may the anthems of the sea,
  That o'er yon isle eternally
Mix with those rival songs of thine,

Lull thee at night, wake thee at morn
  To gaze upon the gleaming sail ;
  And late the spirit-quickening gale
That wafts thee to that other bourn.

LOVE'S ALTAR.

A ROCK, moss-clad, beside a brook,
  A hoary hemlock shading both,
Have made a little twilight nook
  Where lovers come to plight their troth.

And so this rock, so lone and gray,
  Is called Love's Altar, and the tree
Is carved with records of a day
  That from the dim past speaks to me.

It speaks of blighted human hopes;
  It speaks of gloomy doubts and fears,
The failing of earth's firmest props,
  The desolations of the years.

The brook sings on its plaintive song,
  The hoary hemlock sighs above;

But still the wilful wanderers throng
  To the same spot to talk of love.

They read the names and carve their own,
  While the weird branches o'er them wave,
Then go their way to lay them down
  In the embraces of the grave.

THE DEATH-WATCH.

STANDING beside a sick man's bed,
  I felt his pulse and watched his eye ;
At every motion of his head
  I turned in restless sympathy.
The clock ticked in the narrow hall ;
  Outside, I heard the rippling brook
As downward past the garden wall
  Its course among the flags it took.
Damps gathered on the feverous brow,
  And shadows on the wasted cheek
Flickered with lights, that, to and fro,
  In many a pallid, wavering streak
Spoke of the light that is to come ;
  The very leaves upon the oak

Whispered an augury of doom,
  But not a word the sick man spoke.

I heard a ticking like a watch;
  No time-piece had they, well I knew,
Save the great clock; I pressed the latch
  Down with my finger, backward drew
From the hall door, and shut my eyes
  And held my breath; I heard it plain,
Ticking and ticking, though the flies
  Were fluttering on the window-pane,
And louder, in the rising wind,
  The trees moaned and the waters wept,
And the harsh creaking of the blind
  Jarred on the patient as he slept.
Still ticking to my startled ears
  In the old wainscot, on the floor,
And keeping time to all my fears,
  I heard it at the entry door.

I sought it here, I sought it there,
  In every cranny of the room;

But nothing saw I anywhere
  Whence this mysterious sound could come.
I looked upon the sufferer's face ;
  The lips moved, and the eyes rolled wide,
And, wildly fixed on vacant space,
  Without a groan, the sick man died.
The wind wailed on, the great hall clock —
  Through the dull door I heard it yet,
The oak leaves quivered, and the brook
  Sighed to the flags a fond regret ;
But the death-watch, by wall and floor,
  By bed and window, sought in vain,
And on the panels of the door —
  I never heard it tick again.

MY SHIP.

BY J. D. C.

LIST! list! O sea!
My bark, by gentle zephyrs kissed,
Labors through thy clinging mist,
Vernal sea!

Laugh! laugh! O sea!
Golden sunbeams round her lave
As she cleaves thy crispèd wave,
Summer sea!

Joy! joy! O sea!
Wafted by thy fruity gales,
The happy mariner homeward sails,
Autumn sea!

Wail! wail! O sea!
Deep within thy troubled breast
The shattered hulk hath sunk to rest,
Winter sea!

ATARAXY.

('Αταραξία.)

BEFORE it gleams a river wide,
　Enlivened by the snowy sails
That, up and down the brimming tide,
　Are breathed on by the gentlest gales
That ever whispered of the spring ;
　Behind it rise such gallant pines,
That tropic-sunbeams only glance
Through their dim shade, with eye askance,
　To smile upon the jessamines
That weave amid their branches fragrant bowers,
Crowning the forehead of the year with flowers.

And here and there about the woods,
　The holly, with its glossy leaves,
Mirrors itself in silent floods,
　Fanning the violets' breast, that heaves

Responsive to the west wind's sighs.
  Cassena here, magnolia tall,
With flowers as white as angels' wings,
And mistletoe that idly swings,
  Secure in its aerial hall,
And mocking-bird, with ever-varying tone,
Thrilling the tree-top that it perches on;

The wishing-well that bubbles up
  To kiss the image on its breast,
Dimpling its waters to the cup
  That scoops them for the weary guest,
Or planter, resting from his toil;
  The oak, a forest in one tree,
That hides the cedars at its feet,
The old live-oak, — whose arches meet
  Like cycles of eternity,—
Whose long, gray mosses drape it like a shroud,
And breathe sad dirges when the winds are loud,—

These, and the hospitable board,
  The dark-browed soldier, scholar, friend,

Too proud to flatter, and too good to hoard
  One gift of God to any selfish end,
Or hide the light of that bright eye;
  The lady fair, who, like the sun,
Lights up the coldest heart with smiles;
And she, the sister, with no wiles
  Save such as faith and truth put on,
These, — this is Ataraxy; this the Greek
Wandered about the weary world to seek.

To seek and found not; yet on me
  Its lights and shadows softly played,
As, under that ancestral tree,
  The hazel eyes of one fair maid
Shone on me like a gleam from heaven.
  And now, whenever I recall
Thy copses, woods, and blest fireside,
Her image doth before me glide,
  Pervading, beautifying all:
The maiden, bride, wife, mother, seem to be,
Dear Ataraxy, but a part of thee.

ANDREW JACKSON.

A MAN, whose nature loathed a lie,
 Who asked no shield to guard his breast,
But only sought the way to die
 That poets have pronounced the best,
Where men, upon the bloody field,
 Sink foremost fighting for their kind,
Or, living, only live to wield
 A sceptre that can sway the blind.

"Carve on my monument," he said,
 "'Union and liberty are one;'
That he who stands above my head
 May read the text, when I am gone."
Fools scarped the letters from the stone
 That stands above the hero's tomb,
To burn in living hearts alone
 Brighter, until the day of doom.

THE WRECK.

By J. D. C.

The white fog hugs the sobbing seas;
The dripping clouds hang low and black;
The wind, that westward drives the rack,
Whirls the spray through the naked trees:
But high above the ocean's swell
Sounds the hollow boom of the light-ship bell,
The measured toll of the light-ship bell.

She rose up, clad in virgin white;
"Ah me! I cannot sleep," she cried,
And threw the creaking lattice wide
And looked out on the groaning night.
Over the sea, like a funeral knell,
Come the warning notes of the light-ship bell,
The low, sad wail of the light-ship bell.

She starts! A ghostly shape! "Oh, speak!
Why wanderest thou, my soul, alone?"
The wind but answers with a moan.
But hark! A gun — a crash — a shriek!
And over all, with tone so fell,
Booms the weird voice of the light-ship bell,
The haunting voice of the light-ship bell.

"O God! he bids me come!" she cried,
And flew across the yielding sand.
The morning sun, upon the strand,
Shone on two corses, side by side;
And over the swell, like a funeral knell,
Came the mournful toll of the light-ship bell,
The low, sad toll of the light-ship bell.

TO ——,

ON RECEIPT OF SOME SEEDS OF THE GREAT TREE

(*Sequoia Gigantea*) OF CALIFORNIA.

High on the lone Sierra's breast,
  Above the cedar and the pine,
Where eagle never built her nest
  And violet sunsets coldly shine,
Towering above a craggy rock
  And crowned with everlasting snows,
  That glorify its awful brows,
The cypress in the thin clouds shook.

It lived ere Christ was given to men;
  'Twas old before the Cæsars fell;
Nations arose and sank again,
  As bubbles on the ocean-swell

Sparkle and break in the bright sun ;
  Yet, casting o'er the ledge below
  A dusk eclipse and shade of woe,
The mighty cypress still waved on.

Five thousand feet above the seas
  Whose billows wash those happy shores,
While savage kings about its knees
  Scooped the cool torrent as it pours
In fury down the wild ravine,
  Their puny sceptres still it mocked,
  As in the morning's breath it rocked
Its haughty coronet of green.

It looked down on the mountain chains
  Of rifted quartz and links of gold ;
It stooped above the blessèd plains
  Of fruitage, fair and manifold,
And emerald grass upon the slopes
  Smiling in sunshine and in showers,
  And o'er the many-tinted flowers
That symbolize man's dearest hopes.

It saw the Spanish conqueror pass, —
  Cuirass and casque and burning shield, —
It saw the white-robed priest, the mass,
  The victim, scorning still to yield,
And standing with his tawny face
  Uplifted and defiant eyes
  Fixed on those deep and sapphire skies,
Bid welcome to death's cold embrace.

Still those small leaves they sparkled on,
  When came the Saxon conqueror,
His mattock gleaming in the sun,
  The eager Saxon worshipper,
To set up here a gilded throne,
  Even in this Eden of delights,
  And build for Mammon, on the heights,
A mighty empire of his own.

At last, to see the cypress gray,
  A lovely vision of a maid,
Bright as a California day,
  Beneath the immemorial shade

Looked up and blessed it with her eye,
  Stooped down and blessed it with her lips,
  And caught in her white finger-tips
A cone that dropped from out the sky.

A cone, that from the topmost bough
  Fell in the rude autumnal rain,
Destined to be immortal now,
  Its little seeds to live again,
Upspringing, in a distant clime,
  Close by another granite ledge,
  To lift new cones above its edge,
Glooming with twilight more sublime.

THE ICE STORM.

The clouds hung low throughout the livid day,
  Shrouding in mist the evening's loveliness ;
  The wet trees stretched their arms in mute distress
And bowed themselves, as if in act to pray
For respite from the desolating sway
  Of wind and ice ; then came the subtle sleet,
Encasing every form, trunk, branch, and spray,
  Like giants panoplied from head to feet.
Then the wild trumpet blew a dreadful blast,
  And the long ranks of Titans closed in war.
  This one his shield, and that his helmet, far
O'er the wide field in fury from him cast:
  The morning shone ; hushed was the angry jar,
And swords and helms and spears were melting fast.

ANDREW JOHNSON.

WE watched thee, Johnson, through the weary years
Of agony, in which thou hadst a part;
Saw thy wife torn from thee, thy daughter's heart
Wrung with a bitterness too sharp for tears;
When others fled with palpitating fears,
Or kissed the braided lash that gave the smart;
We saw thee, standing up amid thy peers,
Out-facing them upon the public mart
Where men are bought and sold, and 'mid the noise
And clamor of rebellion heard thee cry
Against oppression with a mighty voice,
Whose silvery notes were tuned to liberty;
Therefore the nation now before thee stands
Like Aaron holding up his brother's hands.

WILLIAM A. BUCKINGHAM.

In the old time that gave to Washington
  Its sword to carry, and its glittering shield,
  Connecticut gave Trumbull power to wield
Her banner, with the words inscribed thereon
That Winthrop penned for the brave Puritan;
  The chief and scholar labored in one field, —
The hero called him Brother Jonathan.
  Even so our martyr-chieftain was upheld
By Buckingham, the purest and the best,
  Who gave his time, affections, prayers to the dear
      cause,
With an unswerving faithfulness and zeal,
  To crush rebellion and lift up the laws
Trampled beneath oppression's scornful heel;
Therefore the soldiers bless thee, and the State,
Small in her limits, in her deeds is great.

EDWIN BOOTH.

A GOLDEN sceptre in thy hand, my friend,
  Touches all hearts with tender loyalty ;
  Thy captives ask thee not to set them free,
But love their thraldom ever to the end.
Lo ! millions on thy motion do attend,
  Waiting thy future victories to see ;
And all the muses, supplicating, bend
  To do obeisance to thy royalty.
They see the crown of Richard, Hamlet's cloak,
  Othello's sword, and the brave Cardinal's pen ;
They hear the echo of a voice that spoke
  Of empire and dominion over men ;
And nature calls thee from thy vague alarms
As mothers call their children to their arms.

MILTON.

I HEARD a noise as of all unclean things
  That hurtle in the air; and, looking, spied
  Great flocks of crows and buzzards, far and wide,
Flying one way with dull and laboring wings
To intercept a bird that upward springs,
  Strong-beaked and sinewy-winged and amber-eyed,
His bearing high and haughty as a king's,
  His fiery heart to the great sun allied.
Upward he sped through the black cloud and din;
  No barkings heard I from his airy track;
I watched him till the sunbeams drank him in,
  Then saw the crows and buzzards fluttering back,
While a great crowd below looked up and strove
To learn what bird had killed the bird of Jove.

THE CHARTER OAK.

I STOOD above the spot where stood the oak ;
  Before my eye uprose its mighty frame ;
  The acorns and the green leaves were the same.
I saw the council-fire beneath it smoke ;
Then Wadsworth's footsteps on the silence broke,
  As in its cave he hid those words of flame
Branding upon oppression's weary yoke
  Wrongs of all ages, sins of every name.
I saw beneath it, like a Druid priest,
  Stuart, fond worshipper, before it stand,
Who gazed upon it as the hungry feast,
  Leaning his reverent head upon his hand.
I looked again ; the grass grew green and brave
Above the spot and over Stuart's grave.

www.ingramcontent.com/pod-product-compliance
Lightning Source LLC
LaVergne TN
LVHW011221110826
845150LV00006B/1491
9781425516703